Talking to Your Children About Being Catholic

Peter Kreeft
Bert Ghezzi
Henry Libersat
David Thomas
William Odell

Cindy Cavnar
Robert Barr
Mary Ann Kuharski
Charles Savitskas
Margaret Savitskas

Our Sunday Visitor Publishing Division
Our Sunday Visitor, Inc.
Huntington, Indiana 46750

This work was originally published by Our Sunday Visitor as nine booklets: *Being Catholic* by Peter Kreeft; *Jesus* by David Thomas; *The Mass* by Henry Libersat; *The Eucharist* by Bert Ghezzi; *Reconciliation* by Charles and Margaret Savitskas; *Confirmation* by William Odell; *Mary* by Cindy Cavnar; *Prayer* by Mary Ann Kuharski; and *Death and the Afterlife* by Robert Barr.

Scripture text from *The New American Bible With Revised New Testament,* © 1986 by the Confraternity of Christian Doctrine. All rights reserved.

Sections entitled "What the Church Says About . . ." are adapted from *The Catechism of the Catholic Church.*

ISBN: 0-87973-751-4
LCCCN: 94-68604
PRINTED IN THE UNITED STATES OF AMERICA

Cover design by Monica Watts

751

Contents

Talking to Your Children About . . .

Being Catholic
Peter Kreeft

A Self-Check

You're reading this book because you want to talk to your kids about being Catholic. The very first thing you should do, before you talk to your kids, is to talk to yourself. Ask yourself *why?* Why do you want to do this?

I hope your answer will be something like this: Because I want to help these kids to *be* Catholics, and to know why, and to stay Catholics; to help them to know and believe the truth, and love it, and be nourished by it.

The next thing is to ask yourself, "What do I believe?" You can't share what you don't have.

Do you believe the essential claim the Church makes for herself — that she is the visible institution Christ left on earth to teach with His authority and to give us His body and blood? Or do you pick only those teachings that please you? In other words, do you pick at your food, or do you trust your mother and eat the whole meal?

Can you expect your kids to believe more than you do?

I don't mean that you have to be some sort of super-Catholic yourself before you can talk to your kids about being Catholic. When people call me "a good Catholic," I want to say, "I'm trying to be a good Catholic." But I do *know* that I *am* a Catholic.

Besides checking in with yourself, you should check in with God before you talk to your kids about Him. Before you talk, pray. Before you talk, listen. Let God talk to you.

Ask Him to give you the words He wants you to say to your kids. Put your brain and your tongue at His disposal. You're not in charge here, He is.

The single most important thing you can do for your kids is to love God with all your heart, to give Him your whole will and your whole life, to let Him be your Lord, to say with Mary "May it be done to me according to your word." If you do that sincerely, He will bless your stumbling efforts. If you don't do that, even your most brilliant efforts will be only your work, not His.

For reflection: In doing a self-check about your own beliefs, what conclusions do you come to?

Three Good Reasons to Be a Catholic

Be clear, in your own mind first, why you are Catholic, before you try to share these reasons with your kids.

There are, at least, three very good reasons for being Catholic: Catholicism is true, good, and beautiful.

It's true. Suppose your kids ask: "How do you know it's true? Isn't that just your opinion?"

The answer is simple: "We know the Church is true because it was established by Christ, and Christ is God, and God always teaches the truth. He can never deceive or be deceived."

It is a historical fact that Jesus Christ established the Catholic Church. Church teaching has been continuous for two thousand years. It has never changed Christ's teachings, only expanded our understanding of it, like any growing thing.

Being a Catholic is like having a rich family history. You and your kids should get to know that rich history and tradition. Get books on Catholic saints, art, and history to keep around the house.

It's good. The Church makes saints. In her extreme goodness, she forms sinners into saints. What a supreme example of just how good the Church is!

You can argue with a theologian but you can't argue with a saint. That's why it's so important to have your kids read the lives of the saints. What is a saint? A saint is simply a great lover — of God and neighbor. Saints win the world by their love. It happened two thousand years ago, and it can happen again today.

Saints "sell" to teenagers better than abstract principles. Morality is taught best by concrete examples and stories. It's not so much taught as caught — like a good infection. Saints "sell" to teenagers because saints are great lovers, and teenagers are beginning to explore love. Saints show that love is more than sex, better than sex, happier than sex.

It's beautiful. The Church gives us beauty and joy in its art, music, and liturgy, at their best. But she gives us joy and beauty above all by channeling to us the love of Christ. Christ's love gives us the highest joy possible in this life, because it is the meaning and end of life, union with God.

Get your kids to think about the most important question in life: What is the goal and purpose and end of life itself? Why were you born? Why are you living? What's it all about? The Church exists to answer that question.

Every Catholic used to know the answer strongly and clearly.

- Who made you? God made me.
- Why did God make you? God made me to know Him, to love Him, and to serve Him in this life, and to be happy with Him forever in the next.

That's Lesson One in life. Teach your kids that lesson when they implicitly ask for it, in times of frustration ("Why bother?"), or suffering ("Why did this happen to me?"), or indifference ("What difference does it make?").

Moreover, the Church gives us wisdom, holiness, and joy. These are the three most important things everyone needs. Tell your kids you want the best for them, and the Church has given you the three best things in your life — these three things.

For reflection: What do you think life is all about? What is the purpose of your life?

Teenagers

As everyone knows, teenagers are going through the most traumatic transition time of their lives. Someone defined a teenager as "an adolescent who acts like a baby when you don't treat him/her as an adult." You have to ride their moods like waves. Learn to surf.

Teenagers are especially subject to peer pressure from their friends. If you have any choice about schools or neighborhoods, that should be your first priority for your children: good friends. Teenagers are like half-baked bread — still in transition to finding their own identity and independence. Paradoxically, their way to more independence (from parents) is more dependence (on friends); nonconformity through conformity. But it makes sense. Imagine a hundred people having to wade across a raging river. They'd naturally huddle together. Teenagers' peer groups give the security of being in a group at the same time as the adventure of wandering from the old group, the family. Expect this, as you expect the next wave when surfing.

But beware: Storm waves can swamp you. And there are many storm waves today. Teenagers are exposed not only to a society that peddles deadly temptations to physical and spiritual self-destruction in the forms of drugs, alcohol, violence, suicide, and AIDS, but also to media that propagandize abortion, materialism, and a philosophy of pure hedonism, selfishness, promiscuity, and self-indulgence. Trusting our kids to this society could be like trusting Mary's little lamb to the big bad wolf.

In one important way parents are better off today than a generation or two ago. Teenagers always desire to be rebels against the establishment, and today that means being Catholics, not pagans. The pagans are the establishment. Teenagers will more readily enlist in a cause that they see as heroically rebelling against society, than in established society. They're ready for heroic ideals, even sacrifice. In other words, they're in the market for what the Church offers: the radical message of Christ.

Show them the alternatives. When a movie, or TV show, or their own experience shows them a picture of a ruined family or a ruined life, tell them it doesn't have to be that way. Put alongside that picture the Church's picture, which is not Ozzie and Harriet or the Brady Bunch but Jesus Christ and His radical love — a love that means faithfulness forever.

Rub those two pictures together like flint and steel, and a spark will come. Tell them they have to choose sides. That's what they do in Confirmation.

For reflection: How are the challenges different today for teenagers and parents of teenagers than they were when you were a teenager?

Jesus' Psychology

Jesus was far more than a psychologist. But He used great psychology with people. And we can learn from Him some practical principles about how to talk to teenagers. For everything Jesus was, teenagers naturally want.

Jesus was concrete, not abstract. Jesus was not a scholar but a Savior. Kids are not interested in abstractions but in concrete persons and events. Jesus was always specific. He used concrete images, and told concrete stories, and gave concrete examples. We should try to do the same.

Jesus was always personal, not impersonal. Teenagers are beginning to think seriously about themselves; they are on Jesus' wavelength.

But they don't like to be put "on the spot" personally. You can more easily talk to a teenager about personal things in the dark, or walking side by side, or in the car, rather than face to face across a table or across a room where they feel scrutinized.

Side-by-side (a good image for friendship!) is the happy medium between the extremes of face-to-face (too intimate) or absent-minded and impersonal.

Jesus was relational. His words were like lassos. Christianity is essentially a relationship with God through Christ, a love affair with God. Kids are "into" relationships, especially love relationships.

Jesus was practical and active. He may have been contemplative and mystical in private, but not in public. Kids, too, want to do, act, move, experiment, practice, create. Christianity is a religion to do, because love is something you do, not just think about or even just feel.

Jesus was informal. Kids love to be informal and casual. "Let's sit down and have a little talk" may sound casual and informal to parents, but it sounds like a prison sentence to teenagers. They fear confrontations. We should avoid being stuffy, or superior, or on our "high horse."

Jesus was canny, not naive. You couldn't fool Him. You can't fool kids either. They have very powerful "fakery-detectors." We absolutely have to be totally honest with them. That's why it's so important to begin with some self-scrutiny and ask ourselves what we believe. You can't fake faith.

Jesus talked about Himself. Our kids are more impressed with personal testimony than with anything else. They'll listen to "Here's why I'm a Catholic" more readily than they'll listen to "Here's why anyone should be a Catholic."

———

For reflection: What is your image of Jesus? Is He accessible to you, and are you comfortable in presenting this image to your teenagers?

Timing

In order to keep it casual and non-threatening, timing is important. It's usually obvious when it's a bad time to raise the issue of why you are a

Catholic — when they're engrossed in something else, or under time pressure, or tired, or cranky. But when is it a good time?

The best time is when they open the door a little, when they raise the issue in some way. They would rather choose the topics of conversation than have you bring it up out of the blue. Let them be the verbal initiator and aggressor if possible.

But suppose they don't raise the issue; how do you bring it up?

There's no magic formula. You have to feel your way in, by knowing their personalities. Try to avoid both extremes of pushiness and laziness, saying too much and saying too little.

There are natural opportunities, such as Mass or religion classes. Sometimes moral issues are raised by a TV show, school book, or movie, or a decision in their lives. Sometimes they'll ask for advice on a matter that's partly practical and partly moral, like choosing a job, a club, or a course.

The best way to begin is with a question, not an answer. For instance, "What do *you* think would be the best club to join? What are you looking for? What do you value most?" And when the answer comes, ask again: "And why do you value that so much? How does that fit into your set of values?" That naturally leads to the question "Where do you get your values from?" The Church is the answer to that question.

I know of no universal formulas except honesty, common sense, and prayer. Ask God to guide you and He will, often in ways you don't expect or even recognize.

With some oversensitive and shy kids, there are times when all you can or should do is leave good books and articles around and pray a lot. With others, who are more talkative and open, you may discover that they are longing for deep conversations.

Pre-teens usually find it less threatening to talk about God than teenagers do. So the earlier you open conversational lines, the better.

But all times can be good times because all times are God's times.

For reflection: What is your teenager like? How do you think you could open a conversation with him or her?

Style and Expectations

Teenagers are concerned with style, whether they call it being "cool," "with it," "awesome," or whatever. Adults often fear being "out of it"; consequently, they try too hard and appear artificial. My advice is to ignore style completely and just be yourself.

Use clear and simple language. The test of whether you understand something is whether you can translate it into words of one syllable.

Be straightforward. Don't dance around an issue. Don't be subtle. Teenagers aren't subtle and don't respond to subtlety. Especially, never be sarcastic. Once they feel put down, they turn off.

Avoid long lectures. Be brief and to the point, like Jesus. To do that, you have to find the point yourself first.

All this advice sounds like style, but it's really the way to avoid worrying about style. The most important thing is to just do it. It's like praying, or visiting the sick: What you say is less important than being there and making the effort.

Nobody has perfect style or technique. Nobody totally understands teenagers — not Doctor Spock, not the pope, not the "experts." Only God. And God gave your kids *you*, not Doctor Spock, the pope, or the experts. He doesn't want you to be somebody else, just yourself. Kids respect that.

Expectations. Style isn't simply a matter of "how-to-do-its," but it is also determined by expectations you can have of your kids. What are your expectations?

There is real reason for having high expectations for your teenagers. Teenagers can respond to heroic ideals if their hearts are in it. Having high expectations doesn't mean naiveté. You know they're going to goof, like toddlers learning to walk by falling down a lot. Parents are easily pleased but hard to satisfy when they watch their toddlers toddle. You should be the same with teenagers, who are emotional toddlers.

The ideal for you and them is an unusual combination: both firm and calm, both strong and gentle, both just and loving, at the same time. Teenagers, like everyone else, are looking for exactly what the Church is freely offering: Jesus, the Jesus of the Gospels, who is both the King of the universe and the suffering Servant of the smallest soul.

Picture Jesus. Take a minute to imagine what Jesus would do and say before you speak to your kids. To do this, get to know this Jesus better. Read the Gospels. That will do more for your kids than anything.

So what if you feel clumsy talking to your kids about Christ? He'll make up for your clumsiness. He'll fit Himself into their hearts. You don't have to "sell" Him, just expose them to Him.

For reflection: What qualities or gifts that you bring to your teenagers do you consider most important? What expectations do you have of your teenage children? Do they challenge your teenagers to grow?

Freedom

Your goal is not just to keep your kids Catholic but to have your kids freely *choose* to be Catholic.

If you cared only about their freedom and not about their faith, you'd leave them alone. If you cared only about their faith and not about their freedom, you'd try to manipulate and control them. But since you care both about their freedom and their faith, you try to lead them to the truth.

It's important that you tell them that — that you want them free and you want them true.

Religion is a free choice, a decision. You can influence your kids but you cannot control them. God appointed parents to guide children through jungle paths, not to train animals.

Your kids have to come to God, not to you, to get eternal life. Ultimately, all you can do for your kids is open doors to God; they have to choose to go through the doors. God designed it that way. He gave each individual free will, because only free will makes true love possible.

Kids sometimes think that freedom only means the freedom to rebel, to say "No." Point out to them that the choice to say "Yes" to God and to the Church is just as free and just as much their own responsibility as the choice to say "No."

If everyone must freely choose to believe in Him, are there no "born Catholics"? Should everyone be a convert?

Yes! The Church says we all need conversion. We who were baptized without our choice were also asked to make the choice to be confirmed when we were old enough to make that free choice. We need to reaffirm our baptismal promises again and again, to turn away from sin and deliberately choose God's will.

Those of us who were born into and brought up in Catholic families — so-called "born Catholics" — have a great advantage. It is like the advantage of being brought up in a wise, loving, and intact human family.

That's why you want your kids to choose a deeper involvement in that life they received without their choice in Baptism: because you want the best for them. You should let them know that.

For reflection: How has religion been a decision in your life?

Simulated Conversation: Other Religions

The simulated conversations in this chapter are meant to provide encouragement, increase the comfort level, and spark the imagination of parents in discussing being Catholic with their teenage children.

Kids are naturally interested in the fact that some of their friends believe in other religions, or none at all. This natural interest provides an opportunity to talk to them about why you and they are Catholics.

Bill: Dad, how come most of our friends are Protestants?

Dad: Well, I guess that's because we live in a part of the country where there are more Protestants than Catholics. And it's good to have all kinds of friends.

Bill: Oh.

Dad: Maybe you meant something more important with that question — like why we're Catholics.

Bill: Yeah.

Dad: That's a big question, and a good one. Well, I'll give you my answer if you give me yours. Suppose someone asked you why you're a Catholic. How would you answer?

Bill: I guess I'd say because I was brought up that way.

Dad: That's a cause, but it's not a reason.

Bill: What do you mean?

Dad: I mean, that's the particular family that influenced you, but what are the reasons for anyone to be a Catholic?

Bill: That's a hard question. Why do I have to have reasons?

Dad: Let's take love for example. You want good reasons for loving someone. When I decided to marry your mother, I didn't go into it blind. I knew my reasons — she's beautiful, she's good, and she loves me — and they helped me stand by her and our commitment when things got rough. So I think we should be able to give good reasons for our faith too.

Bill: Okay, if you should give reasons, what are they?

Dad: Okay. Let's start with what Protestants and Catholics have in common that separates them from all the other religions. They're both Christians. That means both believe in Christ and His claim to be the Son of God and the Savior. I'm not a Buddhist or a Moslem or a Jew or anything else, but a Christian, because I believe that.

Bill: Why?

Dad: Because if He wasn't the one He claimed to be, then He was either the most wicked or the craziest man who ever lived. He claimed to be God. If I claimed to

be God, and I wasn't kidding, wouldn't you think I was wicked if I knew it was a lie, or crazy if I believed it myself?

Bill: Of course.

Dad: But nobody thinks He was wicked or crazy. Everyone who reads the Gospels is impressed with this guy and call Him one of the wisest men who ever lived. But non-Christians say He was just a good man. That's the one thing He couldn't be. A mere man who claims to be God is not a good man but a bad man or a madman.

Bill: That makes sense. But why Catholic instead of Protestant?

Dad: Well, the basic answer is that this Jesus founded the Catholic Church. There's an unbroken line that goes back from the Catholic Church of today to Jesus Christ. Protestant churches are only a few hundred years old. They were started by mere men: Luther, and Calvin, and King Henry VIII. The basic reason for being Catholic is that we want to be in the Church Christ founded, and we trust in her traditions and beliefs.

Bill: What do the Protestants believe?

Dad: There are many different

kinds of belief. Orthodox Protestants believe everything in the Bible. Liberal or Modernist Protestants don't believe in miracles or the supernatural.

Bill: What kind of Protestant is Steve?

Dad: He's the kind of orthodox Protestant that's called "Fundamentalist." That means that he not only believes everything in the Bible, but he interprets almost everything literally.

Bill: He seems to be down on the Catholic Church too.

Dad: What does he say about it?

Bill: That we worship the pope, and Mary, and the saints, and even statues.

Dad: That's typical. Most Fundamentalists are quite sincere, but not very well-informed.

Bill: That fits the picture. I don't like to hurt his feelings by criticizing him, though. He seems so sincere.

Dad: We have to judge people's ideas very critically, but we should be very open and accepting to the people themselves, even when they're prejudiced against us. A lot of good people have bad ideas.

Bill: Don't you think we should be open to their ideas too?

Dad: To listen to them, of course. How can you judge any idea fairly without listening to it first?

Bill: Maybe there's truth in all religions.

Dad: Of course there's some truth in all religions. But we can be certain only of the truths revealed by God Himself, and of the religion established by God Himself when He walked on our earth. That's the basic reason why we're Catholics.

Bill: That makes sense. I've got more questions too. Can we talk about them some other time?

Dad: Sure. Anytime. I think God loves honest questioning.

Simulated Conversation: Catholic Morality

Catholic morality is the main reason many Catholics leave the Church or just give up practicing their faith. It's what you do about what you believe. So it's bound to come up in discussions of why (and whether) you are Catholic.

Bill: Dad, why do Catholics have a stricter morality than anybody else?

Dad: Who says they do?

Bill: All my non-Catholic friends. The first thing they think of when they talk about Catholics is strict rules, and laws, and guilt.

Dad: Then they don't know Catholic morality very well. Because the first thing the Church thinks of in morality is love. Jesus said the whole moral law is summed up in the two great commandments; to love God with your whole heart and your neighbor as yourself.

Bill: But the Church does have a lot of laws.

Dad: Sure. They're definitions of love. Love does not kill. Love does not steal. Love does not commit adultery...

Bill: Sure it does!

Dad: Not faithful love.

Bill: Oh. But isn't the Church sort of hung up on sex?

Dad: No, the modern world is, so that's the one part of the whole big Catholic picture they're always thinking about. They don't get the big picture.

Bill: What big picture?

Dad: The Catholic vision of what sex really is. Without that, you're naturally going to misunderstand and misinterpret the rules. The picture of sex as something beautiful and holy and designed by God. That's why there are rules to protect it. You don't make rules about paper clips, but you do make rules about things you care about: life, property, telling the truth . . . and sex.

Bill: But isn't it up to the individual conscience to make its own rules?

Dad: No. That's a misunderstanding of conscience. Conscience doesn't make the rules, any more than your mind makes the rules of mathematics. It discovers the rules. And then it applies them to different situations. It's like measuring. Unless you have an unchanging yardstick, you can't accurately measure different things.

Bill: But everybody has a conscience, right? How are Catholics different?

Dad: We know more. We've got clearer information. You could figure some things out in math by yourself, but your teachers speed that up a lot. Well, the Church is like the teacher of our conscience, and she's got a textbook from God — the Bible — and the authority from God to interpret it.

Bill: But that means we have more rules than other people.

Dad: Not just more rules, more understanding. The big picture, remember. For instance, about sex, the secular world thinks sex is just a biological accident, and we can do whatever we want with it. The Church says it's God's invention, and we'll be really happy in the long run only if we follow the Inventor's instructions.

Bill: But those instructions sound so negative to everybody else. No sex outside marriage, no contraception, no divorce, no homosexuality.

Dad: But behind the negatives is the positive, the big picture. All these things are adulterated sex, not true sex.

Bill: Doesn't that mean the Church condemns a lot of people? Homosexuals, for instance?

Dad: No, not the people. "Love the sinner, hate the sin" — haven't you ever heard that saying?

Bill: But they hate the Church because it condemns what they do.

Dad: But the same Church that says that what they *do* is wrong says they are to be loved. If they reject the Church's authority to say the first thing, they don't have the Church's authority to say the second thing either, the love thing. And then if some people feel like hating homosexuals, what's to stop them? It's a package deal, it all hangs together: love sinners, hate sins.

Bill: But the Church's ideals are so high that it's impossible to live them. It's not realistic to tell people those old ideals anymore. Maybe people could live them in the past, but everything's changed today.

Dad: Not everything. Not human nature. You know, that's really insulting, what people say, that it's impossible to live a moral life today. If we could accept it for 1,900 years, why can't we accept it today? I think the reason people say no one can accept it today is that they've lost the vision, the big picture. They believe we are only animals with bigger brains. They don't believe in God, or God's grace, or human nature as created by God in His image. That's the crucial difference, the big picture. That's what's behind the rules.

Bill: Hmmm! I guess I need to know more about that picture.

Dad: I think you've made a great beginning.

What the Church Says About Being Catholic

The Church is catholic because Christ is present in it. "Where there is Christ Jesus, there is the Catholic Church." In the Catholic Church the fullness of Christ's body, united with its head, is present; this implies that the Church receives from Christ what God has willed for His people: the fullness of salvation.

One comes to this salvation by: the correct and complete confession of faith; full sacramental life; and, ordained ministry in apostolic succession. The Church was catholic on the day of Pentecost and will always be catholic until Christ comes again.

The word "catholic" means "universal" in the sense of "according to totality or wholeness." The Church is catholic because Christ has sent it forth on His mission to all people.

All who are fully catholic are in communion with the Church in Rome, "which presides in love." Those who belong to the Catholic Church are fully incorporated into the society of the Church who, possessing the Spirit of Christ, accept its whole structure and all the means of salvation established in it, and are united within its visible framework with Christ, who governs it through the supreme pontiff and the bishops, by the bonds of profession of faith, sacraments, ecclesiastical governance, and communion. They are not saved, however, even though incorporated into the Church, who do not persevere in love; they remain in the Church "bodily" but not "in the heart."

Outside of the Church there is no salvation. This means that all salvation comes from Christ the head through the Church which is His body. Those who refuse to enter the Church or refuse to remain in it cannot be saved if they are aware that the Catholic Church was founded by God through Jesus Christ as a necessity for salvation.

A requirement of the Church's Catholicity is its mission mandate to strive with its every effort to preach the Gospel to all people. The Church is one, holy, catholic, and apostolic. A profound reality is that the kingdom of heaven already exists in it though it will only be fulfilled at the end of time.

There is a genuine equality of dignity and action among all of Christ's faithful, deriving from their rebirth in Christ. Because of this equality, each contributes according to his calling. There is in the Church a diversity in ministry but unity in mission. The hierarchy refers to Christ's desire that the apostles and their successors teach, sanctify, and govern in His name. The laity share in the priestly, prophetic, and kingly offices of Christ, and play their roles in the mission of the whole People of God, in the Church, and in the world. From both of these groups are drawn those who live consecrated lives. Through the profession of the evangelical counsels, they are consecrated to God and promote the Church's saving mission.

That the Church is holy means *love* is the "soul" of the holiness to which each person is called.

Jesus
David Thomas

Memories and Conversations

Once upon a time there lived a man named Jesus. Almost two thousand years after His departure, His name and many of the important events of His life are known by almost everyone.

He lived when there were no video cameras or tape recorders. In fact, neither newspapers nor magazines were delivered to the front doors of the residents of first-century Jerusalem. Virtually all information was communicated by word of mouth. If you weren't told, you wouldn't know.

It helped that many people had excellent memories. So it will not surprise you to learn that the words and deeds of Jesus were communicated for almost fifty years through ordinary conversation and storytelling around the night fires that lighted the countryside.

It's quite amazing how much was remembered. When various accounts of the life of Jesus were set onto scrolls, what He said as well as the times and places He said these things were filled with specifics with only minor variations in the accounts. Certainly we have in the Gospels good descriptions of the important events of the life and time of Jesus. Archeological research conducted in the last few years has corroborated the original gospel stories.

While the Gospels remain the written bedrock of Christian faith, let us focus on that period before formal writing took place. In other words, let us reflect for a moment on the *way* in which Jesus was first introduced to people. It will help you to appreciate how you can do much the same with your own children.

Many scholars point out that the Gospels use a *story form*. All people enjoy stories. Good stories allow us to reflect on our own lives which are like stories in the making. Automatically we tend to compare other stories with our own. We particularly like stories with happy endings because we want our own lives to end that way.

Characters like ourselves allow us to identify with them. While our lives may not seem to be full of excitement, we connect with exciting characters and, in a sense, live through them.

It is important to grasp this process of identification. If you cannot get into another's story, it will remain separate from your own understanding of yourself and your life. If the Jesus story is told well, the main character will be presented as "one of us." We will be able to appreciate his joys and trials and relate them to our own.

Thus a general rule for the parent is this: Talk about Jesus as a person like us. Recall the concrete details of His life. Stress His goodness but not to the degree that it is unreachable by average good-willed people. Jesus is fully human and our access to His divinity is through His humanity.

Remember too that first impressions are very important. All later ideas and images of Jesus will be built upon that image already there. Do not forget that one of the last things Jesus said to His disciples before His death was that they were, first of all, *friends*. They serve as a reminder to us to speak about Jesus always in terms of friendship and familiarity.

For reflection: How do you feel about thinking of Jesus as a person like you?

Two Special Stories

With younger children the best story to begin with is the story of Bethlehem. In fact, it almost seems that the gospel writers wrote this account with children in mind.

All children readily connect with the birth of a baby. The story of the birth of Jesus is filled with features easily taken in by the child's understanding. Animals come with shepherds and the sky fills with wondrous angels. Eventually wise men or Magi appear with gifts for the newborn. These are scenes filled with happy images and warmth. It is a family story, a story of little ones, a story recalling the great gifts each one has received in life.

It is important that parents attempt to enter the story though the eyes and experiences of children. In reality, many parents have become jaded over the Christmas fiasco because it has become exactly that for so many adults. It is not uncommon for adults to dread the arrival of Christmas with its hectic demands along with a whole set of ambivalent memories. The word of caution here is simple: Don't ruin it for your kids. Be careful not to give them simply *your* Christmas story. Rather, share with them *the* Christmas story of Jesus.

The first simulated conversation on p. 23 revolves around the birth of Jesus.

It may surprise you to learn that when the Church rates its feast days, it places Easter first, even before Christmas. The reason for this is Easter is the day of victory, the day of glory. Jesus was born to live on Easter. It is the first day of Christian history. As the psalmist tells it, "This is the day the Lord has made; let us be glad and rejoice in it" (Psalm 118:24).

Of course, the various aspects of the Lord's life are not to be thought of as in competition with one another. They are all part of a whole. From beginning to end it is all important. But just like our own lives, certain days, certain moments stand out. They seem to have a power of shedding light upon all the rest. And Easter is the great fireball lighting up the sky over all the rest of Jesus' life.

The second simulated conversation on p. 29 revolves around the most important feast of Easter.

For reflection: What memories do you have from your own childhood about Christmas and Easter? How do you make Jesus central to your celebrations of the feasts in your family?

Simulated Conversation:
Once Upon a Midnight Clear

The two simulated conversations in this chapter are meant to provide encouragement, increase the comfort level, and spark the imagination of parents in discussing Jesus and related issues with their children.

A conversation between a dad and his daughter about Jesus and the crib. Sarah is about six years old. They are setting up the family Christmas tree and in the process she opens a small cardboard box filled with little plaster figures. Her eyes widen as she carefully unwraps each figurine.

Sarah: Daddy, look what I found. It's our crib set. Can I set them out?

Dad: Of course you can. Do you know that this is the same manger that we had when I lived with Grandpa and Grandma?

Sarah: It seems really old. Look, here's the baby Jesus.

Dad: Sarah, did you know that Jesus is the most important person who ever lived?

Sarah: Oh, Daddy, you say that about everyone. You told me I was the most important one.

Dad: You are very important, Sarah. And Jesus was very, very special.

Sarah: Do you know the names of these others? I think that one is His mommy, and this one is His daddy. Right?

Dad: Well, that's partly true. His mother is Mary and the man is Joseph, but he's called Jesus' foster father.

Sarah: I don't know what that means. I mean foster father. Are you my foster father?

Dad: No, Sarah, I'm your regular dad, but Jesus sort of has two dads.

Sarah: Oh, I know what that's like. Suzy has two dads, too. Her mother divorced one and she gets Christmas presents from both of them!

Dad: Let me try to explain. Jesus is special because He came to us from heaven. He really is God, but He wanted to live with us. That's why He became a person, just like you and me.

Sarah: You mean Jesus is God? Why did He want to leave heaven?

Dad: Well, Sarah, this is the wonderful part of the story. You know how much you love your little dolly, Marianne?

Sarah: I really love her.

Dad: Wouldn't it be neat if your dolly became a person, just like you?

Sarah: Daddy, that's like the Pinocchio story.

Dad: You're right, Sarah. It is kind of like the Pinocchio story, except the first Christmas story really happened. God wanted to live with us so that we can learn how to live the right way. And the best way to do this was to become just like you and me. So He was born, became a little boy, and eventually grew up and became a man.

Sarah: But what about His daddies? You said He had two of them.

Dad: The real father of Jesus is God the Father. Jesus' life was started by God. Do you remember the story of an angel coming to the young girl Mary and asking her to become the mother of this special person?

Sarah: Did Mary know who this special person was?

Dad: Yes, she did. She was a Jew and the Jews were special people chosen by God long before Mary's time and they were given an important promise. They were told that some day God would visit them and bring them a very special gift.

Sarah: And that gift was Jesus?

Dad: That's right. But it was not an easy choice for Mary because she also knew stories about this person who was to come. And some of those stories said that He would have a hard life and perhaps would have to suffer a lot.

Sarah: So Mary was maybe afraid.

Dad: That's right, Sarah. And to make it all the more confusing, she was told that God wanted her to be the mother of His Son. The Holy Spirit would start the whole thing. The Spirit would work a miracle and Mary would find that new life, the life of Jesus, would begin in her right away. That's why we say in the creed, "conceived by the Holy Spirit."

Sarah: So what about Joseph then?

Dad: Well, it was important for Jesus to have someone help Mary take care of Jesus. It was also important to prevent people from thinking that Mary had done something wrong by not having a husband when she conceived Jesus in her womb.

Sarah: So Joseph wasn't Jesus' real father, but he took care of Jesus just like a good father would.

Dad: Yes, and that's why we think of Joseph as such a wonderful person too. That's why our parish church is named after him.

Sarah: I like Jesus as a baby. But who are all these other people?

Dad: Well, when Jesus was born, we are told there were men caring for sheep in fields nearby. Angels appeared to them and told them about this wonderful good news. So they came to see the little baby and, of course, they brought their sheep.

Sarah: So everyone came to see Him. They must have been happy.

Dad: They were, just like we will be when we share their happiness when we remember the birth of Jesus this year.

Sarah: And who are these other men? They look like they are kings or something.

Dad: In the Bible, Sarah, we are told that some time after the birth of Jesus wise men from a distant country learned about the coming of Jesus. We learn that a very special star of heavenly light directed them to where Jesus, Mary, and Joseph were staying.

Sarah: What are they carrying?

Dad: They brought special gifts for Jesus.

Sarah: So Jesus got Christmas presents too?

Dad: You could say that. It was the way these important people from far away showed their gratitude for this wonderful happening. But you're right. There is a connection between the first Christmas and Christmas gifts.

Sarah: What's that?

Dad: We give Christmas gifts to people we care about in a special way. It's a way we show our love. And the biggest Christmas gift of all was God coming to live with us as a person just like us. God cares about every one of us.

Sarah: Daddy, we should put the crib right in front of the tree so that everyone will see it. I'm going to tell Santa Claus to put my gifts right next to the crib.

The Later Life of Jesus

Children are what developmental psychologists call "concrete thinkers." This means that if you give them an abstract idea, it will enter one ear and exit the other. When sharing the person of Jesus with the young, we have the wonderful advantage of having the four Gospels as our resource books. The brilliance of the Gospels cannot be overstated. As works of ancient literature, they are without precedence.

With that in mind, parents will always be on safe ground if they communicate their understanding of Jesus within the framework of the Gospels. So take advantage of the Sunday Gospel readings used at Mass to start conversations.

Tips on Bringing the Message Home

Read the Gospels together with your children. Read slowly and with feeling and use one of the new translations. Both *The New American Bible With Revised New Testament* and *The Jerusalem Bible* read quite well.

If possible, visit good Catholic bookstores and investigate what materials they have concerning the life of Jesus which are written especially for children. Look carefully at the artwork. Images are important and they have much longer shelf life than do words.

You might also visit a general religious bookstore. Religious publishing, particularly among evangelical churches, is growing at a rapid rate. In the context of Biblical accounts of Jesus, many fine publications are to be found from all the Christian churches.

Also, become familiar with the religion books or catechetical materials used by your children. Showing an interest in this area is always worthwhile.

You might also want to secure some religious art for the home. Quality is much more important than quantity.

Finally, become familiar with contemporary religious music. Young people are deeply influenced by music. Older people can also succumb to its influence, but it's not "cool" to admit this in public. Some Catholic composers, like Joe Wise, have written wonderful music for children.

One excellent starting point is for parents to personally identify their favorite Gospel stories. You might like the dramatic conversation that took place at a well in Samaria (John 4:4-42). You might find ironic humor and meaning in the story of the ingenious people who captured the attention of Jesus by lowering a sick person through the roof into the home where Jesus was staying (Mark 2:1-12). There are also His wonderful words to talk about. He could spin a yarn in the form of parables or straight talk which could set the imagination into overdrive and the mind dancing along the roads of ancient Palestine.

A word of advice about this kind of sharing: Don't try to do too much. Don't try to explain everything. Engage your children in conversation. You are not a teacher but a parent who simply wants to share what is important. A compulsive need to cover all the material usually accomplishes just that: Everything is covered and precious little is *discovered.*

Two special features of the ministry of Jesus can be highlighted for children: Jesus as a wonderful Teacher and Jesus as a miraculous Healer.

One of the most common terms used to describe Jesus is that of Teacher or Rabbi. He taught by both word and example. His classroom was wherever He was. His lessons were directly related to what was happening at that moment.

In one sense, He began to teach at twelve years old when He stayed behind at the Temple to talk with the leaders. Even there, His message was said to have come from God.

His primary learners (or disciples, which means "one who learns") were those closest to Him. He knew that life presented everyone with a confusing collection of ideas and views. He tried to communicate that which was at "the heart of things."

He was not a teacher of useless information, but rather His goal was to teach about how to live a good life, which was a life filled with loving others and being loved by God. Christ's basic teaching was that God wanted to save the world from its sinfulness and reconcile all people to Himself. That showed best how God cares for us (see John 3:16).

This teaching was simple and powerful. Some of His more important lessons were. . . .

- Help each other, especially the poor and the needy.

- Be grateful for life and the favors you receive.

- Pray to God as your friend.

- Don't worry about tomorrow but live today aware of God's care for you.

- Share your possessions with others.

- Respect everyone, especially those who are different from you.

Jesus was also a healer. Many sick and ailing people came to Him in the hope that He would be helpful. He often was. His heart was moved by their faith, and often He showed His love by healing them.

He often mentioned that He was concerned not only about the health of the body, but also the wellness of the spirit. His greatest miracles were those in which He brought the dead back to life. A favorite story for many is the bringing back of His friend Lazarus from death to new life (John 11:1-44). With a smile, we can imagine what it was like to be near the cave-like tomb when Lazarus walked forth; we are told that "a stench" would come from His friend.

Jesus cared about and cured children and adults, friends, and strangers. His miracles were signs of His power and love. They remind us that Jesus always wants what is best for us.

Jesus did not cure all illnesses. He did not bring back to life everyone who had died. Usually His miracles were done to help us understand an important idea. For example, Jesus cured blind people while He talked about our need to see the truth of His words. He was a healer who taught, and a teacher who said words that brought health and vitality to those who accepted His message.

This is the way you want your children to know Jesus — a living and dynamic friend who passionately cares for them.

_____

For reflection: What is your favorite Gospel story? Why does it appeal to you?

Simulated Conversation: The Great Feast of Easter

A conversation between an older son, thirteen years old going on twenty-one, and his mother. This conversation begins with the eating of a purple Easter egg that had accidentally fallen and cracked open on the kitchen floor Easter afternoon.

Tim: Mom, this egg is even purple on the inside. Will I get sick if I eat it?

Mom: Only if you have bad thoughts when you swallow.

Tim: Mom, I'm serious. Sometimes this dye stuff can hurt you. You know, give you cancer or something.

Mom: I'm sure it has been thoroughly tested by the FDA, so don't worry.

Tim: Okay, but if I get sick. . .

Mom: I know. It'll be my fault.

Tim: How come there were so many people at church today? I didn't even get a seat.

Mom: It's Easter and some people only go to Mass on very special days like Easter.

Tim: That sounds like a good idea. How come we have to go every Sunday?

Mom: Well, if you really want to know, it's because we think that every Sunday is a celebration of Easter.

Tim: I think I'm sorry I asked.

Mom: No, it is important to wonder about your religious faith. You're a bright young man and God gave you a mind to use.

Tim: Can I have another egg? But I think I'll take a chocolate one this time.

Mom: By the way, Tim, do you know why we have eggs on Easter?

Tim: Because they're on sale?

Mom: No. It's supposed to remind us of new life. Easter reminds us that while Jesus died, He came to new life on the first Easter.

Tim: I heard once that Jesus really didn't die, but He took some kind of drug and after three days, the drug wore off and He was still alive. Isn't that possible?

Mom: Well, I'm no expert, but it seems to me that so many people would not simply base their faith and their life on some kind of a trick like that. We believe that Jesus really died and overcame the power of death, and through God's power He lived in a new life. That's why we believe your grandfather who just died is now living with God.

Tim: I guess that I agree with you about Grandpa, but I don't see what Jesus has to do with all this.

Mom: Remember that Jesus was also a human being like we are. He died a horrible death, a death we are told was out of love for us, yet His death was not the final act for Him. Through God's love for Him and for us, He came into new life. And we are all promised that same new life, particularly when we live with the same kind of love that was in Jesus.

Tim: You know, Mom, it is hard for me to understand all that. Why does God care about us in the first place? A lot of people seem like real losers. They don't care about anyone but themselves.

Mom: I guess we will always wonder about that, Tim. We are also told that God first loved us. The fact that you and I are here right now should remind us of God's special love for you and me.

Tim: But does God love us even when we're bad?

Mom: I think that's the whole point of Jesus' suffering and death. He died for us to save us from the power sins have over us so we might be restored to a loving relationship with God, self, and others. That's why we should be so grateful to God, and that's why, my son, our family thinks it's important to celebrate Easter every Sunday.

Tim: I figured you would get back to that.

Mom: But don't you see? It's not supposed to be a burden. When someone does something wonderful for you, you want to respond. You want to show your thanks.

Tim: Mom, you're really a good person and I know this all makes sense to you. But it's still kind of confusing to me.

Mom: That's okay, Tim. I struggle with my Christian faith a lot. It's not easy because I'm not sure that people really live with an Easter faith. Maybe that's why one Easter was not enough. We all need reminders.

Tim: Speaking of reminders, did

you forget to give me an Easter present this year?

Mom: What do you think that purple egg was?

The Birth of the Church: Pentecost

Jesus remains present and active in the Church. Remember that Christian faith is not a myth, but it is based on a sequence of historical events. The story of Pentecost is a description of the promise of Jesus to remain with His disciples for all time. God's Spirit, which is the Spirit of Jesus, now takes its place in the Church and in its members.

The danger is to imagine Jesus has left for a long-deserved rest and that He sits next to God the Father in solemn splendor.

This image does not follow from a living faith. Jesus did not leave us. He simply expanded, if you will, His place of residence. That's the underlying point of the Acts of the Apostles. The apostles simply continued what Jesus started. And they could do it well because He was really with them.

We live today in a very secular world. For centuries, we have been told that what's real are only those things we can see and touch and measure. But such an approach to life is terribly narrow. There's much more than meets the eye.

As Catholics, we believe in the Real Presence of Jesus in the Eucharist. The Doctrine of the Real Presence remains a central feature of Catholic sacramental theology. Through God's power the bread and wine are transformed into the body and blood of Jesus. His presence in the gathered Christian community is a sign of God's love and desire to be with God's people. As the community receives Holy Communion, it opens itself to God's transforming presence and power, much like what happened at the first Pentecost.

What is well worth remembering is that the presence of Jesus continues in the Church, especially in its people. When Catholics exit the Eucharistic celebration, Christ is brought into the world. While the Mass may be ended, responsible and aware Catholics leave the church with Jesus in the heart to share that same Jesus with others.

This reminds us that Jesus is not simply a historical person who lived in the rural areas of a Palestinian district called Galilee. He now "travels" with His disciples visiting homes and families, neighborhoods, cities, and workplaces all around the world.

Therefore another aspect of the conversation about Jesus with your children should include something about Christlike actions done everywhere. Of course, at some point in your talk, the focus will shift from Christ in them, to Christ in us, to Christ in me. Then you have really captured Jesus as He intended to come — not just to you but to dwell *in* you and *between* you. As you have heard over and over again, Jesus came for us and for our salvation — yesterday, today, and tomorrow.

For reflection: How is Jesus alive to you today? In what concrete ways has He changed your life?

The Boomerang Effect

In his wonderful book about parenting, *A Good Enough Parent,*[*] the late Bruno Bettelheim shared a powerful insight with his readers. He said that many parents today passed through their childhoods in an unhealthy way. They may have been given insufficient attention. They might have been burdened with unearned feelings of shame. They may have picked up all sorts of harmful ideas about success, intimacy, and the value of human life.

From his decades of research in child development and family life, Bettelheim said that parents are really lucky. They are given a second chance at redeeming erroneous or destructive childhood experiences in themselves by doing the right thing for their own children.

Here's how it works. In the very act of truly connecting with and helping your children, the "child" within you is also helped. In a sense, the relationship of parent and child is pulled into the relational event and all participants are affected. In a word, in doing good for another, one also receives goodness.

---

[*]Bruno Bettelheim, *A Good Enough Parent: A Book on Child-Rearing* (New York: Random, 1988).

Applied to your parental task of sharing the Christian faith with your children, you are given an opportunity to learn again for yourselves. And usually that means improvement.

In Pope Paul VI's profound description of the process of evangelization (a fancy word used to describe the way we share the Gospel with others), he says that not only do parents evangelize their children, but children evangelize their parents (*Evangelii Nuntiandi*, 72).

Many parents will nod in agreement. How often does it happen that children challenge the beliefs and values of parents? How often do children remind their parents of important yet long forgotten ideas? Children can awaken parents to the mystery of life, an awareness that may have gone to sleep years earlier.

Children carry within themselves a wonderful gift from God. It is called the gift of *wonder*. That gift comes alive when the child looks into the cloud-filled heaven and asks where God is up there. It is present on walks and talks when the child's mind darts everywhere with wonder, questions, and curiosity.

Some of those wonder-filled children apparently found themselves one day very close to Jesus. Maybe they had a ball which rolled away from their playfield into the crowd assembled around the Master. We might speculate that suddenly the organized plans of Jesus' disciples for the daily round of miracles and parables were jeopardized. There was only so much time in the day and Jesus had an agenda. And they, the important Twelve, were in charge of crowd control.

Perhaps Peter and Andrew decided that it may be best to encourage the kids to take their ball and get lost. After all, the adults had important things to attend to.

You know the rest of the story. Jesus was not impressed with their priorities. He drew the children even closer, and as He lifted one of them onto His lap, He reminded the adults of what's really important in God's kingdom. So let that be your final thought as you think about how you can allow your children to tell you about their Friend, too.

For reflection: How have you experienced wonder, questions, and curiosity from your children concerning matters of faith?

What the Church Says About Jesus

Jesus Christ came to us from God. He is the Word become flesh. His name in the Hebrew language means "God saves." God is present in the person of His Son who was made human for the salvation of all people, saving us from sin. The word "Christ" means "anointed." It became part of Jesus' proper name only because He accomplished perfectly the divine mission that "Christ" signifies.

Jesus, the Son of God, is a divine person. His title manifests the reality of His eternal preexistence. Jesus is also referred to as Lord. This title expresses a recognition of His divine mystery. The Son of God became a man to save us by reconciling us with God. This means that Jesus is a divine person with a human nature and a divine nature. Jesus is true God and true man. Through Jesus we come to know God's love and become participants in the divine nature. Jesus is for us a model of holiness.

Jesus was born of Mary, a virgin and full of grace. Mary is truly the Mother of God and her virginity is the sign of her unhesitating faith. Mary remained a virgin all her life.

Christ's whole earthly life — His manner of being and speaking — is a revelation to us of the Father. All Christ did, said, and suffered was aimed at restoring fallen humanity to its original vocation of loving communion and fellowship with God.

All Christ's riches are for each and every person. Each one is called to a personal relationship with Christ. Christ did not live for Himself but for others. He died for us that we might be saved from sin. Because Christ is the head of humanity, He can act for everyone. Christ became obedient unto death on a cross. In doing the will of His Father, He atoned for the sins of all people. He was the Suffering Servant foretold by the prophet Isaiah.

Christ's resurrection from the dead is the culminating truth of our faith in Him. This event was God's transcendent intervention in creation and history. This paschal mystery has two aspects: By His death, Christ sets us free from sin; by His resurrection, He opens for us the way to new life. After His resurrection, Jesus remained on earth for forty days. Jesus' final appearance ended with the irrevocable entry of His humanity unto God's glory, symbolized by the cloud and heaven. His ascension establishes His humanity in God's power and authority.

Christ will come again to judge the living and the dead. Christ is Lord of eternal life. The full right to judge the works and hearts of each person belongs definitely to Him as redeemer of the world.

The Mass

Henry Libersat

What If We Had Been With Jesus?

What a wonderful thing it would have been to be with Jesus. If we had walked with Him and talked with Him, if we had been with Him at that first Mass, at the Last Supper — what faith we would then have! But we *are* at the Last Supper! That's what the Mass is all about — it places us in the presence of Jesus Christ and we become active participants in His saving life, death, and resurrection. In Mass we don't just "think back" to the Upper Room and Calvary and the empty tomb. We are there!

This is an important truth that can help us help children understand better what the Mass is all about.

Before we as parents can convince our children about the wonder and beauty of the Mass, we have to be convinced ourselves. The wonder begins with the awareness of what is happening at Mass. The beauty is experienced as we take part in what is happening. Even if the celebration of the Mass has been inadequately prepared, that beauty cannot be taken away.

For reflection: How can you grow in an understanding of the Mass? How can you reflect a positive attitude about the Mass when speaking with your children?

Helping Children Understand the Mass

My wife, Peg, and I have seven children and twenty grandchildren. We've heard our share of complaints from children who didn't want to go to Mass, and we've had many questions asked about the Mass.

We realize children can dislike Mass for various reasons, the most common two being that they don't understand it, and it's "boring."

We'll never forget the time we walked up to the communion rail (before Vatican II), knelt to receive, and then arose and turned around to find our three-year-old, Anthony, crawling out from under the front pew. He had crawled under the pews from the center of the church all the way up to the front. He couldn't stand just sitting there. He had to *do* something — something that made sense to him.

With a little imagination, some quality time, and the cooperation of the parish community, youngsters and even very young children can develop a better appreciation for Mass. Here are some ideas that may help with smaller children.

Playing Mass

For younger children, the Mass has to be experienced more than explained. One way to help them experience Mass more fully is to encourage them to "play Mass." Set up a table and chairs to represent pews. Use dishes for the vessels and dresses or towels for vestments.

I remember "playing Mass" when I was a child. We even had a "high Mass" for Rex when he died. Rex was Uncle Nelson's dog and he had been a good friend. Our parents didn't participate actively, but they didn't discourage us. They even provided towels and dresses (vestments) and dishes so we could have our "Mass." It was an outdoor "Mass," held graveside, something still not in vogue.

I remember those play Masses better than I remember the real ones at church — because at church, when I was a child, no one had anything to do but the priest, altar servers, choir, and ushers.

In your children's play Mass, you could be a member of the "congregation," giving as little direction as possible. Help them take turns acting as priest, server, reader, special minister of the Eucharist, and usher.

Ask them to choose what songs they will sing — and don't be surprised if they end up with something from "The Little Mermaid," "Beauty and the Beast," or whatever is contemporary in film theme songs.

Let the children use their imaginations, and you'll soon find out what they really think the Mass is. Sometimes it's hilarious to hear what they think they hear.

I remember one child asking her parents to pray about the "monkey in swimming." "What monkey in swimming?" they asked. "You know," she replied, "Haily Mary, fulla grace, blessed is the monkey in swimming."

Once you know what they know, you'll have a better handle on what they need to know.

Playing Mass can help little ones learn names of things in the Mass — such as host, chalice, wine, altar, Communion, Gospel.

They are too young to know what proper liturgy is all about, but they will be learning about the Mass at their own level.

Children's Liturgy of the Word

Another good way to help children appreciate and understand the Mass is to "tailor" Sunday Masses to "fit them." Many parishes now have a separate Liturgy of the Word for children. Children in kindergarten through sixth grade are excused after the opening song and go to special rooms where adults go over the Scriptures with them at their level. They come back into the church before (or during) the Creed, usually proudly holding up some picture they have colored with the day's principle gospel theme.

The Mass is not entertainment, but it should not be boring, not even for little children. Worship should be as beautiful and meaningful as possible — for everyone.

———————

For reflection: Reflect on your own understanding of the Mass. At what age do you remember coming to an appreciation and understanding? What were your early experiences attending Mass? What benefits do you see yourself attaining by attendance at Mass? What benefits would you like your children to receive?

Simulated Conversation: Why Does Father Wear Long Dresses?

The three simulated conversations in this chapter are meant to provide encouragement, increase the comfort level, and spark the imagination of parents in discussing the Mass and related issues with their children.

A conversation between a parent and a young child. Jennifer is five years old. She and her mother are returning from grocery shopping.

Jennifer: Mama, why does Father wear those long dresses at Mass?

Mama: Oh, that's a good question, Jennifer. I remember wondering about that when I was a little girl. The dresses are called vestments. Can you say "vestments"?

Jennifer: Sure. Vestments.

Mama: Now, that is the correct name for what Father wears. The vestments go back a long, long way. In a special way, they remind us that our priest is a special servant of Jesus. His long white robe is called an alb.

Jennifer: Mama, sometimes he wears different colors.

Mama: Yes, that's right. Do you know what the colors mean?

Jennifer: No.

Mama: Well, the green represents hope. We all hope in Jesus because he is good and promises to care for us. The red represents God's love — and it also reminds us that some people have died for love of Jesus.

Jennifer: Mama, I like the blue best. What does blue stand for? Heaven?

Mama: Yes, I guess it can mean heaven. But it is also the color that represents Mary, the Mother of Jesus. In the weeks before Christmas, the priest wears either violet or blue to remind us that we are preparing to celebrate the birth of Jesus. And before Easter, the priests wears —

Jennifer: Mama, can we stop for an ice cream?

Overcoming Boredom Among Older Children

Junior high students are no longer "little children," but they are still largely dependent on their parents. They are just discovering their sexuality. They are confused, and tend toward rebellion. Peer pressure and peer approval are very important — because they need to belong. The Scriptures can be applied to this need to belong.

I remember as a youngster how much "family stories" meant to me. I used to sit still for long hours listening to parents, grandparents, uncles, and aunts as they told and retold family stories: How Grandpa Henry had come from France; how Aunt Ida had met and finally married Uncle Nelson; how Cousin Al had killed himself; how the family had suffered but survived the great depression; how Daddy's oxen had beat a neighbor's mules in a hauling contest; how all the family helped Cousin Paul move the old blacksmith shop across ten acres of mud.

As Christians we are the family of God — and each parish is a special family of faith. Parents can help young people "connect" with the Scriptures and the traditions of the faith, especially if the word of God can be applied honestly and specifically to their daily life.

"Boring, boring, boring! We hear the same thing all the time!" Repetition can be deadly or life-giving. Sports heroes are great because they repeat and repeat the movements and strategies fundamental to their sport. Swimmers swim and swim and swim, runners run and run and run — and so on.

We "do the Mass" and "hear the Scriptures" over and over again because they are life-giving. They train us to "run the race" of Christian living. They strengthen us to fight against evil in our own lives and in society. They teach us how to live and to be happy and to help others.

These "repetitions" of the Church have been working for two thousand years. And like sports, every time we "repeat" them, if we work at it, we get better and better.

To help their children identify more personally with Scriptures, some parents hold weekly reflections on the Sunday readings.

It may be helpful, for younger children, to get a good children's Bible or a book on Bible stories. Students in middle school and junior high are usually mature enough to think about the real Gospel — in their own terms.

Perhaps either of the following formats may help.

Looking back to last Sunday. On Monday evening at the dinner table, the family has a tradition of discussing "last Sunday's Mass."

Let's suppose that last Sunday's Gospel was about Jesus calming the storm that was about to swamp the boat. Mother might say, "While Father was reading the Gospel, I thought about how I felt last Friday when I was caught in a traffic jam. I was really upset because I had a million things to do. I guess that was a little storm in my life."

Or Dad might say, "Last Wednesday when I found out that John Walker had been laid off, I was really upset. John and Mary have four children and they've had a lot of sickness. I said a prayer that Jesus would calm John's fears and help him find another job."

Then, as Mother is passing the potatoes, she might say, "Even if there is no big wind and rain, sometimes we feel really troubled or scared." And then she can turn to the most talkative child with this or a similar question: "Sally, can you remember a time when we just knew that God had helped us?"

This provides parents with a wonderful opportunity to show children how God indeed helped the family. The children may need a little prompting. It's hard, at first, to realize how close God is to all of us, but with parental guidance, the children will soon see that God helped the family be strong when Grandpa died, that God helped Fido's leg to heal, and He also helped Mary pass the algebra test.

This application of the Gospel to daily life helps everyone, adults and children, get more out of Mass.

Looking forward to next Sunday's Mass. Pick a dinner time to preview the coming Sunday's Scriptures — perhaps only the Gospel. It could be read by one of the older children. Then each family member could be invited to share one thought that came to mind during response to the Scripture.

If the Gospel is Matthew's account of the beatitudes, you might ask each child to give an example of who in the family lives a specific beatitude well. Sammy might say, "Mama is a peacemaker 'cause when Daddy got mad when I lost his screwdriver, Mama helped me find it." Or, Dad might say, "I think Sally is a very kind person. She is always wanting to help others and she doesn't hold grudges."

Parents have to "give flesh" to the Gospel by helping children of all ages see how the stories, values, principles, and truths relate in their own daily lives.

Maybe it could be fun to make the exercise a guessing game: "What do you think Father Joe will say about the Gospel?" Or maybe ask them to think about how the message applies to school or to the family.

Again, it is a good idea to see what the parish can do to help. Many parishes have a regular Sunday youth liturgy — or at least an occasional one. Many Catholic schools and CCD programs have excellent liturgies for young people. These special liturgies help them relate better to the Mass and then, on Sundays, they bring that experience with them.

For discussion: Can one of these models work in our family? Are we comfortable "talking religion" to our children?

Simulated Conversation: Boring!

Randy is twelve. He's asking questions about the Mass — and he's frustrated.

Randy: But, Mom! It's the same thing every Sunday. Gee whiz! Why can't we say something new once in a while? Every week! The same old thing!

Mom: Randy, how many times have you watched "ET"?

Randy: What's that got to do with Mass?

Mom: Maybe a lot. Come on now, how many times have you watched "ET"?

Randy: I dunno, a lot of times, I guess.

Mom: Yes, about thirty times in the first month we bought the tape. Randy, wasn't that the same old thing over and over again?

Randy: Well, yes, I guess, but it's different. "ET" is a great story.

Mom: So is the Mass. Randy, what would happen to the story of "ET" if we changed some of the facts? What if we had him coming out of the earth instead of space? What if ET was a bear instead of an alien?

Randy: It wouldn't be the same story!

Mom: That's right, Randy, it wouldn't be the same story — and that's the way it is with the Mass. There are some things we can't change because they say exactly what needs to be said. They are a truth that we cannot mess with. Do you see the connection?

Randy: I guess so.

Mom: If you are attentive at Mass and participate, you will understand more. Be patient.

Bringing Your Life to the Mass

Your children need to know that you can see life as they see it.

For example, for the young child, the world is filled with new and exciting things, things wonderful and mysterious, things big and things small.

A young child will be fascinated by a butterfly, a hummingbird, a flower, raindrops, ants, and caterpillars. As the child sees and marvels, she or he is learning about life.

Even at this earliest age, perhaps especially at this age, parents can help children see God in life — and then bring that God-in-life into the Mass.

For smaller children

Look at the world through the eyes of your child. Get down on your hands and knees and see how high doorknobs and steps and chairs really are. See how big chairs are. And if you're game, look at the altar from the eye level of your children. All you can see is the backs of the people in front of you.

Then at home, in your garden or backyard, become like a little child with your child. Link nature with God and with worshiping God. "Mary, look at that beautiful rose. Smell it! Doesn't it smell sweet? God gives us such beautiful things. Tonight when we say our prayers, let's thank God for this rose. And Sunday at Mass, let's thank Him again. Okay?"

Then in night prayer remind Mary about the rose — and in church before Mass begins, mention the rose again, and remind Mary that during

Mass we will thank Jesus for the beautiful rose. Mary may even think of other things to thank Jesus for with a little prodding from her parents.

For the older child

A ten- or twelve-year-old is wondering about other things. Butterflies and hummingbirds and roses are old hat. Now, it's time to stretch those apron strings. Sports, for boys and girls alike, provide ample opportunity for hero-worship and vigorous activity. At this age, some children can move from sports to Nintendo to science with relative ease. Music, astronomy, aerodynamics, and space exploration mesh comfortably with shopping, baseball card collections, makeup for girls, and dirty sneakers for boys. And for some, the opposite sex is becoming more and more interesting.

How can you help them relate their very personal and daily interests to the Mass?

1. Listen to your child talk about his or her interest. Judy is fascinated by the universe. She can name every constellation. She loves to go camping so she can gaze at the heavens. She fantasizes that she flies from one star to another. She orbits planets at will. She goes to the edge of the black hole and back home again.

Go camping with Judy. Look at the heavens with her. As she marvels at the wonders of the universe, in the quiet of the night, let her know you share the same fascination with the universe. Let her talk about "her" universe. Then quietly share "your" universe with her.

"Yes. It's beautiful. It goes on forever. When I look up at those stars, I feel so small and yet so big. I feel part of it all and still I feel different. I guess I began to really believe in God when I began looking up at the stars. God goes on forever. You know, Judy, when I pray, even when I go to Mass, I remember moments like this. When the priest raises the Host and we know that Jesus is right there before us, I remember that He and the Father made all this for us."

Appreciation comes from understanding. Your child will understand God better as he or she comes to know you better. God is filtered through you to them.

2. Using memories of holidays can help children learn more about the Mass. Twelve-year-old Sarah is apathetic about worship, but she really loves Christmas and Thanksgiving at Grandma's.

Sarah's parents may want to help Sarah see the parish as God's family and the Mass as a family gathering. They may want to compare what happens at Grandma's with what happens at Mass.

When they get to Grandma's, there are greetings and hugs and kisses. Everyone is happy to see everyone else. Then, there are quick apologies: "I'm sorry I forgot your birthday." As dinner is prepared, they tell and retell family stories. Everybody pitches in and helps or brings something for the dinner. They set the table. They eat, clean up, and sit down rather full and lazy and spend some quiet time and have a little small talk. They embrace and say their goodbyes.

Sarah may not see it right away, but the Mass follows the same pattern: Greeting, penitential rite, Liturgy of the Word, offertory, preparation of gifts, the Meal, clearing of the altar, reflection, prayer, and announcements and dismissal.

For Sarah, the Mass may be less personal than dinner at Grandma's, but if she can see the parallel, she may well begin to think more positively about the Mass.

Carry the idea through to completion. The Mass brings together God's family. As a family, we are happy to see one another, so we celebrate. We sometimes offend one another and our Father. We apologize. We don't want to forget who we are so we tell our family stories (the Scriptures). We give our gifts to God and the family. We share the greatest of all blessings, the greatest meal we receive, Jesus in the Holy Eucharist. We sit quietly, we pray, we bid one another farewell, we leave — knowing that we will come together again.

One element of Mass we must always emphasize with our children is its mystery. Children and young people are capable of appreciating mystery — they may be even more capable of accepting without question than we!

Human memory recalls the past as past; whereas, in Mass what we as Church *remember* becomes present once again. This element of the Mass is its "Sacramental Memory." We thus gain an experience of the saving and forgiving work of Jesus in the Cross and resurrection in the present.

"At the Last Supper, our Savior instituted the Eucharistic sacrifice of his Body and Blood. He did this to perpetuate the sacrifice of the Cross until he comes again. This is a Sacrament of Love, a paschal meal in which Jesus Christ is consumed, the mind is filled with grace and a pledge of future glory is given to us" (Vatican II, *Constitution on Liturgy*, 47).

For discussion: What does your child remember most about Christmas dinner last year? Who was there? Why were you all together? What stories do the children and parents recollect? Does your Christmas dinner in any way resemble Mass? If so, how?

How to Help Children 'Own' the Offertory and Communion

Children should realize two things from an early age: They can ask God for things they need and they can give God gifts that please Him. The greatest gift we give is, of course, ourselves.

During every part of the Mass we give and receive. Perhaps we most consciously receive during the Gospel and homily and at Communion. Perhaps we most consciously give at the Offertory.

One way to help children understand better how to give is to help them prepare for Mass.

The Offertory

Too often, before the family leaves for Mass, Mom or Dad shoves coins into perspiring little fists and tells the children: "Now this is for Jesus, not for candy. When the basket comes around, give this to Jesus."

Very young children may enjoy the charade, but older children are getting off too easy.

Some parents use Saturday breakfast time for a brief but meaningful reminder of how we give to God at Mass. While at table after the meal is finished, the children receive their allowances. (Older children may have part-time jobs and do not receive allowances, but they should be part of this family exercise.)

The parents chat informally with the children about what they will each do with his or her money. They review the past week, commending children who have done particularly charitable deeds, such as helping Mrs. Smith with her gardening, or running an errand for a busy neighbor, or babysitting for free so a mother could go see her doctor.

The family says a brief prayer, thanking God for their blessings, and promising to give themselves fully to Him.

Then the parents place their offering in the church envelope and each child does the same. This is a good time to instill the idea of tithing — the first tenth to God.

The family is reminded that all gifts of time, talent, and treasure are offered up to God, by and with Jesus, in the Mass. Explain to the children that when the priest holds up the Host and the Cup, they can offer up the gifts they have given all week and the money they have just put in the collection. They are a real part of the Sacrifice.

Making Communion count

I've seen grown men get misty-eyed as their children receive the Eucharist for the first time. The Eucharist is the center of our Faith and Catholic parents struggle to help their children understand and remain faithful to the Eucharist.

We tell children they will receive Communion, that Jesus will come to them in the Sacrament of the Eucharist. In recent years, receiving Communion has become rather matter of fact. While we don't relish the distance we all felt from God in the old days, it is true that God is supreme and we are creatures. Children must be made aware that receiving the Eucharist is the greatest gift God gives us: We are made one with Jesus in a very special way.

But Communion is a two-way street. God gives and we give. As Jesus comes to us, we go to Him. You can tell your children that, at Communion time, they give themselves to Jesus just as they are. It's a great opportunity to explain that God loves them no matter what. The Sunday Gospel may offer wonderful stories that can help you instill in your children a great love and trust for our Lord in the Eucharist — stories such as the prodigal son (Luke 15:11-32), the woman taken in adultery (John 8:1-11), the sinful woman who washed Jesus' feet with her tears (Luke 7:36-50), the good thief (Luke 23:39-43). There is so much evidence of God's love for them.

The more they give of themselves, in trust and love, the greater their capacity to trust and love.

It is important that children understand something about the Eucharist, the Real Presence, the fact that bread and wine are no longer bread and wine, but Jesus in all His humanity and divinity.

It's also important that children learn how their own sacrifices, their self-denial, their dying to self, enables them to receive Jesus with more reverence and meaning.

Larry is on the softball team. He is told over and over again by his coach that the "name of the game is teamwork." Larry works hard to be a good team player.

This means "dying to self." He goes to bed on time. He practices and still gets all his homework done. If he is a good batter, he helps his teammates learn to bat better. He doesn't hog the glory for himself.

Larry's parents can help him realize that what he is doing has a divine dimension. Larry is helping others and that is what God wants us to do. He is, in a sense, killing two birds with one stone — pleasing the coach and pleasing God.

For discussion: Other than the suggestions made here, how can you help your children develop a "giving" lifestyle? How can you help them see God's way in the many things they already do so well — and help them offer these gifts at Mass?

Simulated Conversation: Missing Mass

Patricia is eleven years old. It's Saturday afternoon and she wants to spend the night at Amy's house. She and Amy are good friends. On Sunday, Amy's parents will take them boating. Amy is outside in the car with her mother, waiting to see if Patricia will get permission to join them.

Patricia: Mom, I really want to go. I've never been boating.

Mom: I know, Patricia. It does sound like great fun and I'd like to see you go. But what about Mass?

Patricia: Oh, Mom! It's just this once!

Mom: If you miss Mass to go boating, what kind of example does that give Amy?

Patricia: Oh, Amy knows I'm a good Catholic. I tell her all the time about Mass and how we all go to church.

Mom: Isn't there a way you can go to Mass and go boating?

Patricia: No, Mom. They're

outside right now waiting! Please, just this once! I'll do the dishes every night this week.

Mom: I don't know. I can't help but think there is a better way.

Patricia: They live way across town. If I don't go now, they can't come back to get me!

Mom: Well, maybe I can help. If you stay and go to Mass, I'll drive you over later. Or, if Amy wants to come to Mass with us this evening, I'll drive you both over to her house right after Mass. Then you'll be able to spend the night with her and go boating tomorrow.

Patricia: All right!

Mom: What does this solution do for you and for Amy?

Patricia: Well, it lets me go to Mass and go boating.

Mom: But what does it do for Amy?

Patricia: Well, uh, oh, I guess it gives her a chance to go to church.

Mom: You see, Patricia, this tells us two things. First, difficulties can usually be worked out in a way that is good for everybody. And second, we have to set a good example and try to help other people grow closer to God.

Patricia: Cool! I'll go get Amy.

And Patricia will someday realize that Mom made a sacrifice of her own time to help her daughter make the right decision.

What the Church Says About the Mass

The Eucharist, or as it is called in the Latin Rite, the Mass, is the source and summit of the whole Christian life. The Eucharist contains the Church's entire spiritual treasury, that is, Christ Himself. Through the grace of the Eucharist we share in divine life and the unity of the people by which the Church exists.

In the eucharistic celebration the signs of bread and wine are used. By the use of the words of Christ and the invocation of the Holy Spirit, they become Christ's body and blood. Faithful to the Lord's command until His glorious return, the Church continues to do in His memory what He did on the eve of His passion. He took bread and wine and they became His body and blood in a way that surpasses understanding.

Thanksgiving and praise to God. In the eucharistic sacrifice, the whole creation which God loves is presented to the Father through the death and resurrection of Christ. Through Christ, the Church can offer the sacrifice of praise in thanksgiving for all that God has made.

The sacrificial memorial of Christ and His body, the Church. The Eucharist is a sacrifice because it makes present the sacrifice of the Cross. Christ's sacrifice and the Eucharist are one. The same Christ who offered Himself once in a bloody manner on the Cross is contained and is offered in an unbloody manner.

The Eucharist is equally the Church's sacrifice. The Church, which is Christ's body, pariticipates in the offering of its Head. With Him, it offers itself completely and unites itself to His intercession with the Father for all people. In the Eucharist, the sacrifice of Christ becomes also the sacrifice of the members of His body. The lives of the faithful, their praise, sufferings, prayers, and works are united with those of Christ and with His total offering, and so acquire a new worth.

To Christ's offering are united not only His members still here on earth, but also those already in heaven. In communion with and commemorating the Blessed Virgin Mary and all the saints, the Church offers the eucharistic sacrifice. Also the faithful departed, who have died in Christ and are therefore assured of their eternal salvation but not yet wholly purified, are part of the offering.

The presence of Christ by the power of His Word and of His Spirit. Christ's presence in the Eucharist is what we call *Real Presence.* The ordained priest, in the role of Christ, pronounces the words of Christ. Through Christ's activity, He becomes wholly present in each of the elements of bread and wine.

In the greatness of His love, Christ wanted to remain present to His Church in this unique way. His visible presence while on earth is exchanged for His sacramental presence in the Eucharist.

The Church knows that the Lord comes to us in the Eucharist and is present in our midst, though His presence is veiled. Therefore we celebrate the Eucharist as we wait in joyful hope for the coming of our Savior, Jesus Christ.

The Eucharist

Bert Ghezzi

The Most Important Moment Ever

Many years ago when I was in college, a friend invited me to attend his daughter's Baptism. At the conclusion of the ceremony, the child's godfather made a dramatic gesture I have never forgotten. He held up the baby and said, "What you have witnessed here is the most important event that happened in the world today." Everything that leaders, cities, or nations did that day, he said, paled beside the fact that the little girl had been incorporated into Christ, beginning a participation in divine life that would last forever.

We should have a similar perspective on our children's first Eucharist and on their ongoing reception of the sacrament. With Baptism and Confirmation, Eucharist is a sacrament of initiation. This sacred, sacrificial meal completes our incorporation into the body of Christ and sustains our relationship with God that Scripture calls "eternal life" (John 17:2-3). Other important human events will occur on the day our children receive their first Eucharist, but nothing that happens that day will be as significant as their full initiation into God's life.

Every time our children receive the Eucharist, they participate personally in the most important event that has ever happened. The Eucharist unites them in a special way to the death and resurrection of Jesus. Sacramentally, they transcend the barriers of nature, time, and space to share in that founding moment of the New Creation, when the Lord made us sons and daughters of God.

This perspective should convince us of our responsibility to prepare our children for the Eucharist. We put a lot into getting them ready to live their mere human lives. We should put more into getting them ready to live their divine lives. For example, we spend countless hours coaching our children in reading, writing, and mathematics because without literacy and computation, they will not have very successful human lives. We must put a similar effort into their religious education because Christian living requires faith, worship, charity, and many other realities that our children cannot learn without our aid.

For reflection: Do you put as much effort into preparing your children for their eternal lives as you do into preparing them for their ordinary human lives? What one thing could you do to help your children live the Christian life more fully?

The Power of a Parent's Example

Even with the benefits of supernatural living in view, parents often find it hard to teach their children about the Eucharist or, for that matter, about any other Christian truth. We are afraid we don't understand the Eucharist very well ourselves. We feel inadequate, and are reticent to talk about religious matters at all. These are prominent excuses for our inaction. We find it easier to let the parish school or religious education program do the teaching for us.

Parents would find raising their family Catholic less challenging if things worked that way, but they don't. The parish performs a valuable support service in the spiritual formation of our children, but it cannot do the whole job. In spite of all the competition we have from the glitzy media and the seductive youth culture, parents are still the major influence in the lives of their pre-teen children. Our Christian example does more to shape our children's Catholic faith than anything else. Without it, our children are not likely to apply what they learn from religious educators.

Our children's readiness for the Eucharist depends more on their long-term experience of *our* approach to the sacrament than on instructions in the short term. If we are casual or noncommittal about the Eucharist, or if we have incorrect or immature ideas about it, we can expect our children to share the same attitudes and misunderstandings. For example, we should not expect a child to have a very rich experience of the Eucharist if we approach it as a Sunday obligation that gets our somewhat burdensome religious requirements out the way for the week. However, if we have a mature appreciation for the Eucharist and build our personal and family lives around the presence of the Lord, our children will be inclined to do the same.

Before we talk to our children about the Eucharist, we must pay some attention to the foundations of our own Catholic Christian lives. Unless we have a personal relationship with the Lord, the Eucharist will always be a ritualistic cul-de-sac, instead of a highway leading to a great spiritual adventure. To have that kind of relationship with God involves our taking such actions as:

- Recognizing the Lord's presence;
- Inviting Him into our lives;
- Accepting the new life He gives us;
- Living the supernatural life of His sons and daughters;
- Acknowledging His authority over us;
- Orienting everything around Him;
- Talking openly with Him about our lives;
- Doing what He tells us to;
- Worshiping Him with all our hearts;
- Realizing the sacrificial element in our celebration of the Eucharist (see p. 53, "A Sacrificial Meal").

The place to start up or to renew our friendship with the Lord is a frank conversation with Him. We should tell Him candidly about our needs and wants, repent for our sins, and ask Him to open or deepen a personal relationship with us. Jesus made this promise, "Whoever loves me will keep my word, and my Father will love him, and we will come to him and make our dwelling with him" (John 14:23).

Food for Thought

We can grow in our appreciation of the Eucharist through study of Scripture. Reflect, for example, on these words of Jesus: "Amen, amen, I say to you, unless you eat of the flesh of the Son of Man and drink his blood, you do not have life within you. Whoever eats my flesh and drinks my blood has eternal life, and I will raise him on the last day. For my flesh is true food, and my blood is true drink. Whoever eats my flesh and drinks my blood remains in me and I in him. Just as the living Father sent me and I have life because of the Father, so also the one who feeds on me will have life because of me" (John 6:53-57).

Other Scriptures about the Eucharist:
The First Eucharist, Luke 22:14-20.
Jesus' Last Discourse, John 13-17
Jesus' Sacrifice, Hebrews 9:11-10:25
The Appearance on the Road to Emmaus, Luke 24:13-35

A Sacrificial Meal

What is this Holy Eucharist that is the foundation of our lives? Jesus Christ instituted the Sacrament of the Holy Eucharist at the Last Supper. He took bread and transformed it into His body. He took wine and changed it into His blood. He commanded His apostles and us to eat His body and drink His blood.

This Eucharist makes present Christ's suffering and death on the Cross, His resurrection from the dead, and His promise of eternal life. Christ died and rose to save us from our sins and death and give us everlasting life here and hereafter.

The Eucharist makes present the saving power of Jesus from His Cross and resurrection. That is why we call it a sacrifice. The Eucharist makes possible our communion in that grace. That is why we call it a meal. The Eucharist is a *sacrificial meal*.

A sacrifice with no communion would mean we do not share in Christ's saving graces. A communion with no sacrifice means we just have a meal with no saving power. Jesus is present as our crucified and risen savior. Jesus is present as our Living Bread. It is with this whole Jesus we have our prayerful conversation.

For reflection: Are you the kind of Catholic Christian you want your children to be? What is your attitude and practice regarding the Eucharist?

For prayer: Lord Jesus, send the Holy Spirit to help me talk to you about my life. I want to come to know you better. Please help me to appreciate the Eucharist more and to build my life around your presence. Show me how to introduce my children to you and how to raise them as faithful Catholics.

Talking to Your Children

A good example must include not only what you do, but also what you say. A silent witness is not sufficient. Children may observe their parents' faithful reception of the Eucharist and completely misinterpret it. If you don't speak to your children about your love for the Lord and your experience of the Eucharist, even your best example may appear to them to be empty formalism. Your participation in the most important event ever may look to them like you're simply going through the motions because you have to.

If you don't already, you should start talking about God and His ways in the course of ordinary family conversations. Your children should know how important your relationship with the Lord is and how you came to know and serve Him. Talking about God is a means of acknowledging His presence in your family and creates an appropriate context for talking about the Eucharist in the midst of your daily routines.

Opportunities to speak to your children about the Eucharist range from casual conversations through formal lessons. Informal occasions can include:

- Answering a child's questions;

- Explaining your behavior, when a child is apt to miss or misunderstand the spiritual dimension of your actions; and,

- Making object lessons that draw truths about the Christian life or the Eucharist from everyday occurrences.

The simulated conversations that follow this section give examples of each of these three opportunities. Watch and listen for these opportunities, for they pop up all the time. Dispose yourself to seize upon such chances, even if they interrupt or inconvenience you.

In addition to these spontaneous exchanges, you can plan to have conversations at specific times, such as at breakfast, supper, or bedtime. These can be more or less organized discussions. For example, you could consider the needs of your child, and make a list of topics you want to cover this week in short bedtime talks. Or you could choose a book of stories or lessons, and spend five minutes at supper each evening working through it.

Reading the Bible or telling Scripture stories are excellent occasions for parent-child talks. These more formal inputs can act as triggers to draw out your children. Always give them a chance to ask questions or to say what they are thinking.

For reflection: When during the next week might you have a chance to talk to your child about the Eucharist? Decide to start a conversation at one of those times. Assess your child's understanding of and attitude toward the Eucharist. Make a list of topics that you think would help the child appreciate the Eucharist more.

Tips for Talking With Kids About the Eucharist

1. Talk to your children about your own experience of the Lord and the Eucharist. Your personal sharing will present the Lord to them as someone they should get to know.

2. Tell your children about the Eucharist in your own words. Try to be as correct as you can, but don't fuss about it. Right now they need your witness more than they need theological exactness, which — though important — can come later.

3. Have real conversations with your children. Keep "lectures" to a minimum. Get the children talking by asking them how they feel about a topic or what they think about it.

4. Listen carefully to what the children say or ask. To paraphrase Yogi Berra, you can hear a lot just by listening, which enables you to assess where the children are spiritually and how well they are responding to your conversations about the Eucharist.

5. Watch for opportunities to talk about the Eucharist as they come up in everyday circumstances. This helps teach the children that the Eucharist is not just a Sunday observance, but an everyday reality.

6. Build more formal discussions of the Eucharist and other Christian truths into your family life. Having regular Bible studies or instructional sessions shows the children that their preparation for the Eucharist is important to you.

7. Do not hesitate to talk to children about topics that might seem too difficult for them to grasp. Open and stretch their minds by giving them the full picture. Some truths that they don't understand now, they will discover later. Others will remain mysteries for them, as they do for us.

8. Trust the Holy Spirit to guide you and to ensure that you will do a good job in talking to your children about the Lord and about the Eucharist. We receive a special grace through the Sacrament of Matrimony that equips us to raise our children in the faith.

Simulated Conversation: Why Can't We Do It?

The three simulated conversations in this chapter are meant to provide encouragement, increase the comfort level, and spark the imagination of parents in discussing the Eucharist and related issues with their children.

A conversation between a parent and a seven-year-old child that is initiated by the child's question . . .

Joe: Mom, you know at Mass, the priests offer the bread and wine to God?

Mom: Yes?

Joe: Well, how come only the priests do it? Why can't we just do it ourselves?

Mom: Good question, Joe. Let me see. You remember that the bread and wine are *our* gifts to God?

Joe: Yes.

Mom: Well, the priest is our special representative. He prays over the gifts. He asks God to let them become the body and blood of Jesus. Then he gives the gifts to God for us — representing us — and receives them back to share with us.

Joe: But why can't we just give the gifts ourselves?

Mom: Joe, there's a way you can give the gifts — you can offer yourself to God. In fact, when the priest is offering the bread and wine, you should tell God you are offering yourself to Him. You remember we talked about that before.

Joe: Yeah, like the people who get to carry up the bread and wine.

Mom: Our family could volunteer to do that some time. Would you like to?

Joe: Maybe. What if I dropped the bread?

Mom: You wouldn't drop it, Joe. I heard Dad say you had "good hands" when you were playing football last week. Okay. A big part of the Eucharist is your giving yourself to God. But only the priest has the power to say "this is my body," to change bread and wine into the body and blood of Christ and to give the gifts to God.

Joe: I'd like to get me some of that power.

Mom: You know, Joe, that can be arranged.

Joe: I know. If Jesus calls me to be a priest.

Mom: That's right. Now wouldn't that be great?

Simulated Conversation: Put Your Attention on Jesus

A simulated conversation between parent and child based on a parent explaining his or her behavior. Missy is riding home with her Dad from Mass.

Dad: Missy, remember when you tried to talk to me during Mass, and I said, "later"?

Missy: Yes.

Dad: Well, this is "later."

Missy: I just wanted to say that the boy in front of us looked just like Joe.

Dad: Except his ears were a lot bigger. Let me explain why I wouldn't talk then.

Missy: I know. You were praying.

Dad: That's right. I was praying.

The time after communion is special. Do you know why?

Missy: Yes, Jesus is there with us.

Dad: You got it. After we all receive the Eucharist, Jesus is present in a very special way: giving us strength, uniting us to each other, making us more like Himself. So we should put all our attention on Him, just being glad that He's there, and not be talking to each other. Okay?

Missy: Okay. Dad, are we going to stop for donuts? I want one with sprinkles.

Simulated Conversation: Real Dogs Can't Talk

Simulated conversation between parent and child based on a parent making an object lesson. Kate and her mother have just finished viewing an animated cartoon feature.

Mom: Kate, what would you think if Ruffles could talk — like the dog in the movie?

Kate: It'd be cute. It'd be interesting.

Mom: Do you think it could ever happen?

Kate: That's crazy, Mom! Real dogs can't talk.

Mom: What would you say if it could really happen?

Kate: It'd be great!

Mom: I was hoping you'd say, "It'd be *super!*"

Kate: Uh oh! Is this turning into one of your "lessons"?

Mom: You guessed it, honey. I want us to talk for a minute about the word "supernatural." It will help you understand something about your first Eucharist. Okay?

Kate: Okay, but it better not be boring.

Mom: A little hard to understand, but not boring. You already understand that it would not be natural for Ruffles to talk.

Kate: Right.

Mom: And if she really could talk, she would be doing something only people can do. She would be doing something "supernatural" for dogs.

Kate: You lost me.

Mom: Well, if Ruffles could talk, she would be doing something "above" her doggieness, "above" her nature. Something "super."

Kate: She would have some kind of special power?

Mom: Right. Good thinking, Kate. A talking dog would be supernatural. It would have to have supernatural powers to do something only people can do. Now what if you and I could do something only Jesus could do?

Kate: Would it be "supernatural"?

Mom: Right, again. You're good,

honey. On their own, people can't do the things God can do. If they could do something Christ does, then it would be "above" their nature as humans. Supernatural. They would have to have supernatural power to live like God, to do something only God does.

Kate: Are we done yet?

Mom: Stay with me just a little longer, Kate. I'm getting to the main point. Do you remember what we said happened to you at your Baptism?

Kate: Father Bob dunked me in water.

Mom: And as a result, you got new life, a share in God's life. And when you receive other sacraments like Eucharist and Confirmation,

well, they give you more of God's life, and they give you new supernatural powers to do some things Jesus does.

Kate: Like what?

Mom: The main thing is that when you receive the Eucharist you can worship God the way Jesus worships Him. When we celebrate the Eucharist we are one with Jesus and we worship with Him in a way that's very pleasing to God.

Kate: Mom, this is getting boring.

Mom: Okay, Kate, I know this is difficult stuff. We'll talk about it again. For now just remember that the Eucharist gives us the power to do some things God does, something supernatural.

Conversation Starters: Four Eucharistic Themes

You can help your children understand and appreciate the Eucharist if you relate it to their lives. Familiar ordinary realities that kids already value can be conversation starters for exploring the meaning of the Eucharist. You can also interest your children in the Eucharist by participating in some everyday activities that parallel the Eucharist. You can use these activities to illustrate the meaning of the Eucharist in ways that will capture your children's attention.

Spiritual Food. If your kids are like mine, one of their main interests in life is food. How many times a day do I hear, "What's for dinner?" or "Isn't there anything good to eat (read: junk food) around here?" Our kids also understand that in addition to causing pleasure, food is essential as nourishment for our lives.

So, food is a natural starter for conversations about the Eucharist, since it is a ritual meal. Here are some ways food can help you talk to your children:

- The Eucharist is a meal. On the table of the altar, Jesus feeds us with bread and wine, His body and blood.

- Just as food nourishes our bodies, the Eucharist is spiritual food that nourishes our soul.

- The bread and wine are signs that tell us the Lord is nourishing us spiritually.

- Unlike other signs — stop signs, for example — that can't cause us to do anything, the bread and wine of the Eucharist cause what they signify. They nourish us in our spirit; they cause us to grow in Christ.

Suggested activity: Volunteer with your child to serve a meal at a soup kitchen or other facility that feeds the hungry. Not only will this simple service be a chance to talk about spiritual food, but it will teach the child an important duty of living in Christ, the obligation to reach out to the poor.

Real Presence. Friends are a high priority for your kids. They like to be with friends and share as much of life with them as possible. Your children's experience of friendship can be a launch pad for talking about the Eucharist, the sacrament in which Christ is present to us and shares His life with us. Some possible lines for conversation are:

- We like to be around friends and our love for them grows when we're with them.

- Jesus called us friends (see John 15:15) and in the Eucharist made it possible for us to be with Him.

- Jesus is really present in the Eucharist under the form of bread and wine.

- When we celebrate the Eucharist and spend time in Jesus' presence, our love for Him grows.

Suggested activity: Take your child to church to make a visit to the Lord in the Blessed Sacrament. You can get as close to the tabernacle as possible. Encourage your child to be with the Lord in silence. You can also take turns praying out loud, talking to Jesus in your own words.

The Eucharist

Sacrifice. Christ's sacrifice on the Cross was the offering of His body and blood to the Father as gifts for the salvation of the world. In the Eucharist we offer the Father this gift of Jesus. It is the greatest gift we can give the Father and we receive abundant blessings because of this. Kids like to give and to receive gifts. Exchanging gifts symbolizes our desire to be united with others. Offering sacrifice is the normal human way of giving the gift of ourselves to God, so that we can become one with Him. You can use the concept of gift-giving to help your children understand the sacrificial element of the Eucharist. Here are some points to make:

- We give gifts as a sign of our giving ourselves to people we love.

- Friends like to share our gifts to them with us — like candy or toys — as a way of uniting themselves to us in love.

- In the Eucharist, we give bread and wine to God as signs of our giving ourselves to Him. God unites our self-giving with the bread and wine. Through the action of the priest, the Holy Spirit transforms the bread and wine into the body and blood of Christ. This act makes present the sacrifice of Jesus Christ and its divine powers of salvation for us. When we receive Communion, we are united with Jesus and transformed by His saving power into Him. When we eat ordinary bread, we change the bread into ourselves. When we eat Christ's Eucharistic Bread, He changes us into Himself by giving us a deeper share in His divine life and love.

- God accepts our gifts (bread, wine, ourselves) and changes them by uniting them with Himself. Then He gives them to us to share in Holy Communion.

Suggested activity: Encourage your child to give a gift to someone he or she loves, perhaps Mom or Dad, a grandparent, brother, sister, or godparent. Help the child earn the money to buy the gift by paying him or her for chores, so that the gift really represents a personal offering of self. Suggest that the gift be something that could be shared, such as candy, food, or a game. Then the recipient can complete the circle by sharing it with the child.

Celebration. We have parties to celebrate events and anniversaries, and kids like them because of the food and the activities, like games, dancing, and song. Eucharist is a celebration of the most important event ever and parties can help us talk to our children about it. You will find the following themes helpful:

- We get together with friends to celebrate events like weddings and graduations, to remember events like birthdays, and sometimes to thank someone who's been good to us.

- At parties, we celebrate with special foods and drinks, and we do things like sing and dance to express how we feel.

- The Eucharist is a celebration. We gather with friends to remember the death and resurrection of Jesus.

- The Eucharist is a thanksgiving celebration for what God has done for us in Christ.

Suggested activity: Allow your child to plan a party for a birthday or anniversary, or for some other event. Or involve your child in preparations for a party that you are holding. Use the experience as a chance for conversations about the ties between celebration, remembrance, giving thanks, special foods and activities and the Eucharist.

The Center of the Home

When our children were very young, Mary Lou and I made two decisions that have shaped our family life. We agreed that our family would always worship together at Mass on Sunday and that we would make the Church year come to life in our home.

We made these choices because we wanted to have Christ as the center of our home. We wanted everything in our family's life — every relationship, activity, interest, and problem — to revolve around Jesus and to be touched by His gentle influence.

Sunday Eucharist together. We worked to make Sunday worship together a highlight of the week. We taught the children that participating in the Eucharist enabled us to share in the death and resurrection of Jesus, so that they would not see Mass as a mere legal observance.

We did everything we could to involve them in the celebration. We explained the Mass and the Eucharist to them, encouraged them to watch and listen attentively, and to pray and sing heartily. For example, we have taken time on Saturday night to review the Scripture readings to help the kids get more out of them, and we sometimes have a little discussion about the readings or homily in the car on the way home.

Mary Lou and I have also done a variety of things to make Sunday worship special. For example, we have everyone dress as nicely and neatly as possible to express respect for Jesus in the Eucharist. We also do it because we know that when people are neatly dressed they regard events with more seriousness.

We have also made Sunday morning together more pleasant by having a nice breakfast, serving family favorites such as topsy-turvies (biscuits in orange/applesauce) or complementing standard fare with donuts or coffee cake. With four sons and a sports-enthusiast mom, conversations at these meals have often focused on the hot contests of the weekend, but now and again we talk about the most important event ever.

Celebrating the Church year at home. Bringing the liturgy into our personal lives has been a goal for Mary Lou and me ever since our college days. We have long desired to have our little family live out the big drama of salvation history as it unfolds in the Church year.

Over the years we have adopted a few simple celebrations to engage our family's participation in the key events of the life, death, and resurrection of Jesus:

- We anticipate the coming of Christ around the Advent wreath. We talk with the kids about the coming of Christ in history, His coming to us personally and sacramentally in the Eucharist, and His ultimate coming at the end of time.

- We bless the Christmas tree and read the Christmas story before exchanging gifts. We speak about God becoming human, and humans becoming God, a reality we experience regularly in Eucharist.

- We help the children select penances and positive actions to express repentance during the Lenten season. Lent is a preparation time for new Christians to receive Baptism, Confirmation, and Eucharist at the Easter Vigil. So we take opportunities to talk to the kids about their own Christian initiation and about renewing their fervor for the Lord in the Eucharist.

- Celebrating the Passover Meal as it was in the time of Christ is the only elaborate event in our family's liturgical repertoire. During a celebration of this sacrificial meal, at which the Jews remember their deliverance from captivity, Jesus founded the Eucharist, our sacrificial meal that recalls our deliverance from the captivity of death. Mary Lou and I have always used this Christian Passover Meal as a means of instructing all of our children about the Eucharist, especially our first communicants.

Family observances are so much a part of our life that if we were to skip one inadvertently, the kids would miss it and request that we do it.

Every child has responded differently to our efforts to make the Eucharist the center of our homes, some with more enthusiasm than others, but they are all growing up with a realization that the Eucharist is very important to our family.

For reflection: Which of your family traditions provide good occasions for growth in faith? What new family observance would provide more opportunity for faith growth?

What the Church Says About the Eucharist

The Eucharist is the source and summit of the whole Christian life. The Eucharist contains the Church's entire spiritual treasury, that is, Christ Himself. He is our Passover and living bread.

Thanksgiving and praise to God. In the eucharistic sacrifice, the whole creation which God loves is presented to the Father through the death and resurrection of Christ. Through Christ, the Church can offer the sacrifice of praise in thanksgiving for all that God has made good, beautiful, and just in creation and in humanity.

The sacrificial memorial of Christ and His body, the Church. The Eucharist is a sacrifice because it makes present the sacrifice of the Cross. Christ's sacrifice and the Eucharist are one. The same Christ who offered Himself once in a bloody manner on the altar of the Cross is contained and is offered in an unbloody manner.

The Eucharist is equally the Church's sacrifice. The Church, which is Christ's body, pariticipates in the offering of its Head. With Him, it offers itself completely and unites itself to His intercession with the Father for all people. In the Eucharist, the sacrifice of Christ becomes also the sacrifice of the members of His body. The lives of the faithful, their praise, sufferings, prayers, and works are united with those of Christ and with His total offering, and so acquire a new worth.

To Christ's offering are united not only His members still here on earth, but also those already in heaven. In communion with and commemorating the Blessed Virgin Mary and all the saints, the Church offers the eucharistic sacrifice. Also the faithful departed who have died in Christ and are therefore assured of their eternal salvation but not yet wholly purified are part of the offering.

The presence of Christ by the power of His Word and of His Spirit.
Christ's presence in the Eucharist is what we call *real presence*. This makes
the Eucharist a totally profound reality. The ordained priest, in the role of
Christ, pronounces the words of Christ. Through Christ's activity, He
becomes wholly present in each of the elements of bread and wine, in such a
way that the breaking of the bread does not divide Christ.

In the greatness of His love, Christ wanted to remain present to His
Church in this unique way. His visible presence while on earth is exchanged
for His sacramental presence in the Eucharist. In His eucharistic presence,
He remains mysteriously in our midst as the One who loves us and gave
Himself up for us, and He remains under signs that express and
communicate His love.

The Church knows that the Lord now comes to us in the Eucharist and is
present in our midst, though His presence is veiled. Therefore we celebrate
the Eucharist as we wait in joyful hope for the coming of our Savior, Jesus
Christ.

Reconciliation
Charles and Margaret Savitskas

The Reality Facing Us

All the signs are telling us that people are just not comfortable with the Sacrament of Reconciliation. The official Church has made an enormous effort to change that by updating the way this sacrament is celebrated. The New Rite of Reconciliation, published in 1973, introduced face-to-face confession with the opportunity of a more personally meaningful celebration. But the results were dismal. Today, with exceptions here and there, fewer people, not more, make use of this sacrament. Most kids who receive First Reconciliation do not return until Confirmation. Parochial school students are regularly shepherded to the sacraments, but the practice does not continue after they graduate.

Something more is obviously needed. The groundwork has been done. The theology has been revitalized, and the rite has been revised. The "something more" is rediscovering Reconciliation as a life-giving element in Christian life, especially family life.

There is a way to do this, which holds much hope for the future. It revolves around how parents "talk" to their children about reconciliation. Simply, the key is this: Find the essence of this sacrament — honesty, sorrow for wrongdoing, making up, forgiveness, and making amends — in real life. Look for these elements in your life as a family. They are there! Sin is a fact of life. So is reconciliation. When we recover this truth we will become more aware of our need for the Sacrament of Reconciliation, more open to how it can nourish our lives, more interested in celebrating the reality of God's love, forgiveness, and healing in our lives. Then we just might be able to keep our children from drifting away from this "awkward" sacrament.

For reflection: How do you feel about the Sacrament of Reconciliation? What attitude do you want to convey to your child?

Teach Your Children Well

We were working in the yard one Saturday afternoon when we overheard our young neighbors arguing. In exasperation, seven-year-old Ryan hurled this volley at his four-year-old brother: "Am I to take it, then, that you don't appreciate all the things I do for you?"

You know he didn't make that up all by himself. Mom or Dad must have thrown that one around a few times. And there it was, floating through the neighborhood from the mouth of their elder child and now, even worse, in print.

Kids pick up everything from their parents. What parents do and how they communicate with one another and with their children on a day-to-day basis are ordinary ways messages get across to kids. It is crucial for parents to know how to use these channels effectively.

In addition, life occasionally presents parents with "teachable moments" with their kids, situations in which we can directly share our insights and beliefs. Some foresight can help us recognize those occasions and strengthen our position in dealing with our children.

In this chapter, we will take a look at several ways you can "talk" to your children about Reconciliation. We will discuss:

- Actions and attitudes in the home that promote reconciliation;

- How you can help prepare your child for First Reconciliation.

For discussion: With your child (or with your whole family), identify several specific attitudes, interests, and beliefs that you share. Ask your child to tell you about a time he or she remembers well when you taught or helped him or her understand something. (Both parents and children may discover some very interesting things in this process.)

Reconciliation in the Home

At root, Reconciliation is all about love. To reconcile means to restore to friendship or harmony, or, in other words, to re-establish the positive relationship that existed before. The family is built on love — the love of parents for one another, the love of the parent for child, the love of brothers

Elements of Reconciliation

At home	In the sacrament
Honesty	Examination of conscience
	True sorrow
	Rejection of sin
	Intention to sin no more
Own wrongdoing	Confession of sin
Making up/ repair damage	Penance
Say "I'm sorry"	Act of contrition
Being forgiven	Absolution

and sisters, the love of God. Reconciliation in the family means to restore the harmony, and, if necessary, the love too.

Forming your child's image of God

Try this exercise: Picture your child doing the one thing that is most angering or upsetting to you. Then imagine your own reaction to that behavior. How have you responded or how would you respond to your child? Read on only when you have the whole scene clearly in mind.

Whether you acted with anger and force or acted with patience and balance at such highly charged moments like this, you are forming your child's image of God. For all of us, our image of God, even in adulthood, is formed mostly in family relationships, especially by the way parents react with children in both the ordinary and intense moments of life.

How you deal with your child will have a strong effect on your child's image of God. So, ask yourself: If my child goes to God in confession, will God be expected to respond with anger and punishment, or with understanding and peace? Which God would my child want to approach?

Not a knee-jerk, but a nurturing response

In your response to the mental exercise posed above, you may have said that on good days you would handle the situation admirably. At other times, however, you might blow it! That is probably true for most of us. But there is such a thing as a pattern. At some time or another, we all get into a rut. When we are offended or annoyed by something, we do the knee-jerk reaction, anger or force. If we are to develop new responses to old situations, if we are to do the right thing at the difficult moment, we need to make some changes. The old stand-by responses won't meet the need when we are trying to make a difference in the way we live this sacrament in everyday life.

In most of the examples we'll be talking about, the key for parents is a nurturing attitude. It's a Christ-like way of tailoring your responses to your kids in a variety of situations, including the difficult, emotionally charged ones. Undoubtedly, nurturing takes a lot more time than the knee-jerk response. But the results are usually worth it.

Work for honesty in the home

In living the elements of Reconciliation in our everyday lives, there is a basic tenet: Everybody plays by the same rules. Like nurturing, it is something that comes up all the time.

Truth and trust are two elements in the Sacrament of Reconciliation. From them flows a clear, honest conscience. Parents set the basis for conscience formation by how honestly they deal with their young children. They set the basis by the premium they place on trust and truthfulness.

Whenever you talk with your children, you need to be truthful with them so that they know the relationship is honest, inviting them to be honest in return.

The fact is that little children are easy to deceive. But there comes a point when they know they have not been dealt with honestly. They may be too young to say it in words, or even be consciously aware of the connections going on inside them. They simply soak up reality. And yet, from their experience as children, they will carry into their adult lives a commitment to trust and honesty or an attitude of distrust and dishonesty.

Make forgiveness real

How children experience forgiveness and reconciliation in the home will also shape their ability to forgive and to accept forgiveness. In most homes, it's typical for parents to make kids say they're sorry when they have done something wrong. And that's good. But there is a flip side. This is another place where parents have to play by the same rules. Parents need to be ready to apologize when they have wronged each other or wronged their children in some way. For instance, when we come home from work after a particularly bad day, it is easy to come down hard on the children for trivial things. If this ever happens to you, the best message you can send to your children is admitting you were wrong and saying you're sorry. For example: "I'm sorry I was angry with you. You didn't do anything wrong. I was really still angry with my boss at work and I was taking it out on you. Forgive me."

Some children growing up learn that the "magic words" are "please" and "thank you." And those words do indeed sometimes get magical results. But there are other words that are even more powerful. They are "I'm sorry," "I forgive you," and "I love you."

Children need to take advantage of the many opportunities offered in normal family living to say and hear the magic words. They need to say and hear "I'm sorry." They need to forgive and be forgiven. They need to love and be loved.

Peace be with you

Parents can also "talk" to their kids in a powerful way by using the signs and symbols of our Catholic faith. They can be a strong positive influence in the preparation for Reconciliation. For example, before tuck-in time at night, simply make the Sign of the Cross on the child's forehead. Don't be afraid to say the words: "I bless you in the name of the Father, Son, and Holy Spirit."

When we do this as parents, we should be aware of a couple of things. First, by the fact that we are baptized Christians, this is a real blessing. It is a sign and symbol we can use and the Church encourages us to use. Second, giving a blessing sends a message to the child. It says, "I love you, God loves you, and everything is all right between us. So you can sleep peacefully tonight."

Later, when the priest blesses your child in absolution, the gesture will be a familiar reassurance of God's continuing peace in his or her life.

For discussion: As you watch TV with your children, be on the lookout for scenes where deception looks better than honesty, or where dishonesty works to someone's advantage. Does the truth come out in the end? Does the deception cause other problems?

Helping Your Child Toward First Reconciliation

First Reconciliation means just that — *first* Reconciliation. As such, we do not presume that we will teach our children beforehand everything they will ever need to know about Reconciliation. It means that we are making a good beginning, that formation and growth should be ongoing. Secondly, First Reconciliation implies that it is a practice that will continue afterward, that it is meant to become a lifelong practice.

One hot afternoon while we were at the playground with our children, we heard a girl about eight years old spitefully teasing a younger girl and calling her names. When the little girl's mom confronted her about it, she denied it. We recognized her as a girl from our parish who had received First Eucharist and Reconciliation that year. Perhaps she had not experienced a deep transformation or conversion because of her sacramental encounters. Kids don't get perfect overnight. So after you've done your best, be patient with yourself and your child. Leave the rest to God, who has a lifetime to work with each person.

In the meantime, try to help your child realize that everyone does wrong sometimes. What is important is to get up when we fall, to keep trying, to try to do better next time.

Scanning for storms at bedtime

As your child approaches First Reconciliation, a good practice to begin at bedtime is talking over how things went for your child during the day. It is a matter of checking to see if there are any storms brewing in your child's life. If things went badly or somebody upset him or her, this is a perfect time to pray together to be able to let the pain go and forgive the person involved. Or, if it turns out that your child has hurt someone else, your prayer should acknowledge the wrongdoing and ask God's forgiveness. At the same time, help your child decide how he or she will seek forgiveness of the offended party, or how to make amends.

Make Your Home Within Us

What do you want for your children? Most of us just want them to be happy in whatever walk of life they enter. In our hearts we know that's not going to happen without God. Life needs to draw its energy and meaning from the spiritual, or it withers. We know that where Christ is, there also is peace and happiness. In Scripture, Jesus tells us if we love Him and keep His word, the Father will love us and together they will make their home within us (John 15:23).

So we pray:

Lord, we love you and keep your word. Help us when we falter. Make your home within us and grant us and our children your peace.

Distinguish between sins and mistakes

When our son Adam was five years old, I mentioned that I wouldn't be home for dinner that evening because I was going to give a talk to a group of parents. In his best interview style, he grilled me for the facts, all leading up to the final question: "Daddy, what's a sin?"

I remember instantly praying to say just the right thing and not blow this "teachable moment." I knew the first impression he got from me on this one would probably stick.

So I said, "You know when you spilled your milk the other day, and I yelled at you? Well, even though I got really angry, what you did was just an accident. I got upset because we had just had the carpet cleaned, not because you did something wrong.

"Now, remember when you were playing with your building blocks yesterday? Pretend that your little sister came by, as she often does, and knocked over your beautiful tower. What if you got mad at her and pushed her down? Then Mom hears her crying and asks you what happened, and you say she fell. Well, there you have two sins. First, you push your sister down, and then you lie about it to Mom. No accident there. That would be hurting somebody else on purpose and then lying to squirm out of the problem. That's sin.

The Prodigal Child and the Loving Parent

When we read the Parable of the Prodigal Son (Luke 15:11-32), we usually see the father as God. But the father is also you as parent. As your children grow older, what is God's word for you in this parable?

(1) Let your children make mistakes and learn their own lessons. Let them go. Wait and trust that they will return by the right path. Be sure to let them know that they can make things right again.

(2) Love your children unconditionally. Accept them for who they are. Strengthen the positives, challenge the negatives. God wants them to grow and change, not into entirely different people, but to fully develop into the wonderful people they are.

Give your children all you have. Lavish them with love, concern, patience, prayer, hope, time, waiting with arms open wide, words of welcome, and happy celebration.

"And while we're on the subject, my getting mad at you when you spilled the milk was a sin. Like I said, I was thinking about the carpet, but that's no excuse. I'm sorry I yelled at you, and I wish I hadn't done that. I love you, kid."

When you put it like that, it seems so crystal clear, doesn't it? But sometimes, we unconsciously send double messages to kids when we say one thing and communicate something else by our behavior. Most parents know very well that there is a big difference between sins and mistakes. In angry or emotional moments, however, we often send messages that can blur the difference that we only yesterday so clearly explained. If we react with lots of emotion and anger at the spilled milk, for instance, we have already sent the message that this is really bad, perhaps worse than sin. The hard job for parents is to save their anger for real wrongs, not the inconvenient annoyances of child-rearing. But that takes practice and foresight, because it comes from how we live, not how we talk.

There is yet another dimension to the definition of sin, the divine dimension. It is very important to communicate to our children that when we sin, we not only harm a relationship with another human being, but we also weaken our relationship with God. Consequently, when we reconcile, we wish to restore our human relationships as well as our relationship with our loving Creator.

Kids must own their wrongdoing

One of the forms nurturing takes in terms of Reconciliation is helping your kids own their wrongdoing.

One day we were at the lake with some of our in-laws and lots of young cousins. Everybody was enjoying the water, until. . . .

It seems Matthew was standing on the shore, still dry, when Jenny sent out an enormous splash that drenched him. Simply put: Matt didn't like it, and he slugged her.

For parents, this is the fork in the road. You always have two choices about how to respond. You can crack down and, in effect, cut off communication, or you can try the nurturing approach.

In this case, Matthew's dad was horrified (and humiliated), and he immediately took control. He seized Matt by the arm and dragged him screaming to the cottage. He delivered a short, loud lecture, laced with threats, and concluded with: "I don't ever want to see you do that again. Now you sit in that chair until we go home, and don't move!"

That is, of course, an immediate solution to an immediate difficulty. But it only creates a new set of problems. It teaches the child very definitively how to use power and control responses in dealing with other people.

Let's take a look at how a nurturing solution might work. Matthew's dad calls him to the side of the cottage where they can talk privately. "What happened out there?" he begins. Matt looks up with a twinkle in his eye, thinking, "He doesn't really know I punched her." His father squelches that illusion: "I saw you hit her. Why did you do it?"

"She splashed me."

"Was that any reason to hit her? It's like going after a fly with a hammer. It's just too much power for the problem."

"But the water was cold, and it made me mad."

"What else do you think you could have done?"

[Silence.]

"Why couldn't you just splash her back?"

"She was already wet."

"Well, why couldn't you just laugh it off?"

"Maybe I could have done that."

"What else could you have done, maybe?"

"I could tell her how I felt."

"That's a better idea. But that's not what you did. So now you'll have to do something to make this right. I want you to go down and tell her you are sorry . . . not just words, I want it from your heart. You were wrong and you have to own it."

Parents must own wrongdoing too

Of course, we can't expect our children to own their wrongdoing if we refuse to do so. It's like the time the fifth grade teacher called Mrs. McCarthy to talk about her son Charlie. His behavior was consistently inappropriate, rude, and distracting to the class. The teacher suggested a meeting to see if they could work together toward a solution. Mrs. McCarthy responded by saying, "My son isn't like that," and added that she felt the teacher was doing nothing engaging or interesting in class. The problem was theirs, not hers. Wherever the truth lay, it was clear that this parent was not going to acknowledge her son's wrongdoing. Without that, the situation would not be easily healed. Had Mrs. McCarthy been able to do that, her son would have heard loud and clear that he had to own his own wrongdoing.

Fix the problem

Teaching your children to say they're sorry is one way of helping them own their wrongdoing. But words are cheap. And words are not enough when there is property damage. If your child breaks someone's bicycle, for instance, saying "sorry" just isn't enough. In this case, nurturing means accepting the inconvenience and the cost of repairing the bike. In our fast-paced world, by taking the time and money to fix the problem, a parent is communicating another very clear message: It is really important to make up for wrongdoing.

Break the patterns of wrongdoing

Reconciliation is a healing sacrament. If we bring the elements of Reconciliation into our daily lives, we will also bring healing. It is one thing to help your kids own the wrongdoing. It is another to heal by breaking the patterns of wrongdoing. Here is one example and what you can do.

As you already know from experience, everyone takes his or her turn getting into a bad mood. This particular day my son was in a grumpy mood. I wasn't sure if it was just a mood or if something was bothering him, but he seemed to be a bit short with his little sister. By the tone of his remarks, he seemed to be looking for trouble.

My first thought was to put some distance between them and send each of them into separate rooms. But that didn't seem quite fair, so I decided to try something else.

"Come here, Adam," I said to him, in a soft voice. "Look me in the eye." As soon as he did, I said, "You know I love you with my whole heart and soul?"

He said, "Yes."

"You know how we try to walk with Christ in this family?"

He said, "Yes."

"You know we all get a little short from time to time?"

He said, "Yes."

"This time I want you to let your anger go. It's your enemy. And let Christ's peace be what's in your heart."

I didn't know what would happen. But to my delight, it absolutely worked. He was fine from that moment on.

I believe it worked because I spoke out of love and truth, two of the major elements in the Reconciliation sacrament.

For discussion: Discuss the possibility of making a family agreement to never go to bed angry with another family member. What would it take to do that and hold to it?

Simulated Conversation:
What Will Father Think of Me?

The two simulated conversations in this chapter are meant to provide encouragement, increase the comfort level, and spark the imagination of parents in discussing Reconciliation and related issues with their children.

A conversation between parent and child preparing for First Reconciliation . . .

Mom: Well, honey, your First Reconciliation is coming up next week. How do you feel about it?

Allison: OK, Mom.

Mom: Are you comfortable with it? Are you sure you know what to do?

Allison: Yeah, Mrs. Davis explained everything. And Father Ron came to class and talked to us and answered all our questions.

Mom: So you're not worrying or wondering about any of it?

Allison: Well, there is one little thing —

Mom: Yes?

Allison: Well, Father Ron likes me. He thinks I'm, you know, good, like, all the time. What if I tell him about something bad I've done? What if I see him after Mass or on the playground?

Mom: You think maybe he'll change his mind about you? That he'll think less of you?

Allison: Yeah, I'll be so ashamed!

Mom: I know what you mean. I guess we should be ashamed of our sins. But, at the same time, we have to remember two things. First, the priest is there as a friend. He takes the place of Jesus. Second, Jesus loves you — no matter what you've done. If you come to Him and say you're sorry and ask Him to forgive you, He will.

Allison: I know, but what about Father Ron?

Mom: Father Ron is bound by the seal of confession. He honors the confession as a sacred secret. He loves you and identifies with God's forgiveness of your sins.

Allison: Are you sure?

Mom: Yes, absolutely. Now, anything else?

Allison: Mom, will you come with me that day?

Mom: Of course I will, honey. I wouldn't miss it. And we'll go out for ice cream afterwards, okay?

Allison: Great! Thanks, Mom.

Actions and Words Speak Loudly

In the area of reconciliation, as in so many other situations, our own behavior as parents is really what "talks" to children. Our actions help form their image of God. Our attitudes help form their conscience. Our responses help kids know what is a sin and what is an accident. Our actions help kids own their own wrongdoing, or break patterns of wrongdoing. Our actions show that truthfulness and forgiveness are two of life's key values.

What about our words? They tend to clarify and support all the other messages our lives have been giving along the way.

When both our actions and our words make the elements of reconciliation part of our everyday life, we will be living the sacrament in our lives. Only then, as a people, can we reclaim the Sacrament of Reconciliation as the channel of God's life and healing it is meant to be for us.

For reflection: Forgiveness is one of life's most important values. If everybody you know lived by this value, would it make a difference in your life?

Simulated Conversation: Do We Have To?

A conversation between parents and an older child on the way home from Mass on Sunday morning . . .

Mom: I see here in the bulletin that there will be a reconciliation service Thursday evening. I think it would be a good idea if we all went.

Darrell: Aw, Mom! Do we have to?

Dad: I think your mother is right.

Darrell: But why? Do we have to?

Mom: Well, for lots of reasons. First of all, it's Lent and we're supposed to be getting ready for Easter, for resurrection. We can't rise up if we're all bogged down with sin and guilt and bad habits.

Dad: I second that! Anyway, how long has it been since we've been to confession. Too long, that's what. I'm sure you can think of something to confess, Darrell.

Darrell: It's not like I'm goin' to hell, Dad. Anyway, I try to say I'm sorry whenever I'm wrong. Why do I have to go to church with it?

Mom: This is the way we can be sure of receiving God's forgiveness. It's the best way to make things right again with God and with other people. And we also receive God's grace to do better and avoid sin. Do you see what I mean?

Darrell: Yeah, maybe.

Dad: Okay, that's settled. I want everyone back in this van on Thursday at quarter to seven. That means you too, Dee Dee.

Dee Dee: Aw, Dad. . . .

What the Church Says About Reconciliation

The greatest gift for each Christian is to know and accept God's love. This relationship of new life begins in Baptism, that time of the first and fundamental conversion. However, the new life received in Baptism does not eradicate human frailty and inclination to sin. Only with Christ's grace does each Christian move toward constant conversion, holiness of life, and ultimately eternal life. Thus, conversion is an ongoing challenge.

Sin is an offense against God, a rupture in our relationship with Him. It is, as well, a harming of our communion with the Church. For this reason, conversion brings about God's forgiveness and reconciliation with the Church as expressed and accomplished through the reception of the Sacrament of Penance.

Thus, conversion is first of all God's grace working within us. God gives us the grace to begin anew. It is only in seeing God's love and truly recognizing how extraordinary it is that we can see how unsatisfying and burdensome sin is. The human heart can never be satisfied with a life oriented away from God.

The Sacrament of Penance offers the opportunity to be converted again and to recover the grace of justification. A person approaching this sacrament must do so with contrition (that sorrow of the soul), recognition of sinfulness, and a resolution not to sin again. Confession follows contrition. Through confession, sins are admitted to the priest who represents Christ. The penance given is known as satisfaction. In this, sinners recover full satisfaction by doing something to make amends.

The greatest fulfillment a person can ever truly know is to be united to God and others through charity. The Sacrament of Penance provides the opportunity of encountering a God of mercy. Regular confession helps form our consciences and strengthens us against evil tendencies. This healing which comes from Christ Himself strengthens us spiritually. It allows us to join with God in the highest friendships and be restored to ecclesial communion here on earth.

Confirmation
William Odell

The Story Begins

Imagine the scene. The infant Church had just experienced the stoning of Stephen, Christianity's first martyr. A severe persecution of the Church began, led by a man named Saul, who unbeknownst to him was about to experience a shock-therapy conversion. But presently he was busting into homes and dragging out men and women and having them imprisoned for believing in Jesus Christ.

Electricity was in the air. There was a magician named Simon who was astounding the people of Samaria, so much so that the people called him the "Power of God." But there were other things happening that caught Simon's eye. The apostle Philip was preaching about the kingdom of God and baptizing people in great numbers. Simon added himself to the number. Peter and John were sent for so that the newly baptized might receive the Holy Spirit. Simon was so impressed by the "trick" of conferring the Spirit by the laying on of the apostles' hands that he offered them money and said, "Give me this power too, so that anyone upon whom I lay my hands may receive the Holy Spirit" (see Acts 8:18-19).

No doubt about it, that action which was central to what eventually became known as the Sacrament of Confirmation had powerful significance in the beginning days of the Church. In our present age of buying and selling, Simon's gesture surely speaks.

Over nineteen centuries after Simon, a seventy-seven-year-old man, Pope John XXIII, surprised the world and the Church's leaders by calling an ecumenical council, Vatican II — arguably the most significant religious event of the twentieth century. He said it was time to open the windows and let some fresh air in, invite a new movement of the Spirit, a new Pentecost.

This chapter is about how Spirit and power are manifested in the Sacrament of Confirmation. It is about how we can discern and measure how we are growing in the life of the Spirit. It is intended to help you, the parents, talk to your teenage children about a religious experience that is rooted in a flame ignited almost two thousand years ago . . . and still burning brightly today.

Let's Get Acquainted With the Holy Spirit

There would be no Sacrament of Confirmation without the Holy Spirit, so it is important to understand who the Third Person, this often "forgotten person," of the Blessed Trinity is.

In John 3:8, we learn a fundamental attribute of the Holy Spirit. "The wind blows where it wills, and you can hear the sound it makes, but you do not know where it comes from or where it goes; so it is with everyone who is born of the Spirit." This "airy" quality of the Holy Spirit is something that can be understood by reflecting with your teenagers on life's surprises. How many times do we come to decisions or move in directions not knowing what motivated us and how we got there? We can say, "It just happened!" or we can wonder if we were given a nudge. The Spirit is transparent and unpredictable, by human measure.

Ask teenagers who is the most outstanding non-family member in their lives: a sports figure, movie or TV star, musician, teacher, political or religious leader, etc. They are impressed by what they read about the person, a bit more moved by seeing the person on TV. If they could be in the same room, the impact would be greater. If they could touch the person, it would be electric. If they could *know* the person, it would be "awesome." That takes someone or a special set of circumstances to make it possible for us. It works the same way with Jesus.

Jesus Christ has redeemed us, but without the Spirit who testifies to Him (see John 15:26), our faith may never grow beyond the "read about" level. It is the Holy Spirit who makes the *person* of Jesus accessible and knowing Him in a personal way "awesome."

Agnostics admire Jesus' character. Those of non-Christian religions reverence Jesus for His wisdom. Nominal Christians are impressed with His power. Spirit-filled Christians hunger for His life-giving word and to know Him. So when we call the Spirit "the giver of life," it is a statement that should be understood quite literally.

Teenagers are quite relationship oriented, a fact that is sometimes intimidating for them and petrifying for you as parents. They seek more than to admire; they want close friendships. Temperamentally, at least, they are disposed to the beginnings of a vital and personal relationship with the Lord. Whereas a young child may exhibit unquestioning trust in Jesus (child-like faith), a teenager can exhibit trust in Jesus filled with questions. The Holy Spirit enables the teenager to mature in that relationship.

The Holy Spirit is not some vague and fuzzy shadow of God, but God in us. "Do you not know that you are the temple of God, and that the Spirit of God dwells in you?" (1 Corinthians 3:16). Although transparent, the Holy Spirit is not without personality. A name that is given to the Holy Spirit, Advocate (see John 14:16; 15:26), has meaning. Watch a TV show portraying a lawyer in a courtroom drama, and draw a parallel between the Spirit and a legal advocate. Like an advocate in a courtroom, the Spirit will argue the case for us (and for the whole Church) by teaching, leading, defending, and imploring. "As proof that you are children, God sent the spirit of his Son into our hearts, crying out, 'Abba, Father!' So you are no longer a slave but a child, and if a child then also an heir, through God" (Galatians 4:6-7).

Teenagers can understand that relationship by thinking of grandparents or aunts or uncles who often intercede for them with their parents, or guidance counselors who intercede for them with their teachers. Like these people, and parents too, the Spirit counsels, consoles, and enlightens us.

For discussion: If you could meet Jesus face to face, what would you want to say to Him? ask Him? do with Him? (Suggestion: Do this together with your son or daughter or as part of a family activity. You might additionally want to encourage participants to imagine the circumstances of a face-to-face encounter: where, when, how, who.)

You Will Receive Power

During dinner some evening, you might want to brainstorm with your teenager concerning what type of people are powerful. Whom does your teenager know who has power and how is that power shown? When is power respected and when is it not respected?

Just before His ascension, Jesus told the apostles, "You will receive power when the Holy Spirit comes upon you. . ." (Acts 1:8). Do we think those words were only for the apostles and for their successors, but not for "ordinary" Catholics? "Amen, amen, I say to you, whoever believes in me will do the works that I do, and will do greater ones than these. . ." (John 14:12). Do we believe it?

These are crucial questions, and the answers will reveal much about our attitudes concerning the Holy Spirit and the Sacrament of Confirmation. The questions are crucial for teenagers, for often they feel powerless.

What is power? It is the means to make something happen, whether by position, skill, wealth, or circumstance. The power that Jesus is talking about is power to continue God's creation and bring the will of God to bear upon people's lives. A parent raises a child to respect other people. That is power. A teacher inspires a passion for learning in a student. That is power. A parish alleviates hunger and homelessness in the community. That is power. A teenager persuades a classmate to get off alcohol or drugs. That is power. It is power rooted in God's grace, God's love for us.

As is true with all the sacraments, the Sacrament of Confirmation is the outpouring of God's love for us. That love is expressed distinctively in this sacrament through the gifts the Holy Spirit brings to us. God's grace, in the Person of the Holy Spirit, gives us power. But power for what?

It is the power to be Christ-like in our daily lives. At various times, St. Paul advises the early Church communities what that means. With your teenager, you can read one piece of advice in 1 Thessalonians 5:14-18. It may sound like a tough agenda. So what's the key? The key is responding to the presence of God in us. It is not what we do by ourselves, but how we cooperate with God's plan that makes the difference. Do not stifle the Spirit. And the gifts of the Spirit . . . let us open them.

For discussion: Who are the most powerful people you know? What makes them powerful? (Suggestion: Use this discussion to illustrate how power can be seen in kindness, gentleness, and humility, along with such "muscular" qualities as willpower, intelligence, and physical strength.)

The First Thing to Do With a Gift Is Open It

Recall with your teenagers occasions they received birthday gifts and Christmas presents. Did they just greet the occasions with yawns? Or were they filled with anticipation and excitement? Did they put the gifts aside and plan to open them another day? Or did they open them right away, ripping the paper off with no thought of recycling it?

The analogy applies to the gifts of the Spirit. Pentecost is traditionally thought of as the birth of the Church and each commemoration of Pentecost in the Church's liturgical year as a birthday party. In the Sacrament of Confirmation, the candidate receives gifts.

In the confirmation rite, the bishop extends his hands over the candidates and prays: "All-powerful God, Father of our Lord Jesus Christ, by water and the Holy Spirit you freed your sons and daughters from sin and gave them new life. Send your Holy Spirit upon them to be their Helper and Guide. Give them the spirit of wisdom and understanding, the spirit of right judgment and courage, the spirit of knowledge and reverence. Fill them with the spirit of wonder and awe in your presence." These are the seven gifts of the Holy Spirit.

- **Wonder and awe in the presence of the Lord** (fear of the Lord) helps us to honor the Lord and make Him number one in our lives.

- **Reverence** (piety) helps us to be grateful to God for His blessings and to respect all of God's creation.

- **Courage** (fortitude) helps us to boldly live by and proclaim the Gospel.

- **Right judgment** (counsel) helps us to make decisions guided by the Holy Spirit.

- **Knowledge** helps us to put our trust in the Lord and to have confidence in His teachings.

- **Understanding** helps us to see the Lord and His ways more deeply.

- **Wisdom** helps us to make judgments based on God's love.

We are strengthened in these gifts in the Sacrament of Confirmation. But what is the evidence? How do we know whether we have opened the gifts? How do we know that we are responding to the Spirit in us? Ask your teenagers how they know they can trust someone. A friend listens, keeps a secret, is there when needed. To put it colloquially, "the proof is in the pudding."

"By their fruits, you will know them" (Matthew 7:16). In Galatians 5:22, we have a listing of the fruits of the Spirit: love, joy, peace, patience, kindness, generosity, faithfulness, gentleness, and self-control. The Church has added three more: long-suffering, modesty, and chastity. These are the qualities that will be evidenced in the person who is responding to the Spirit within.

It would be simplistic and self-defeating to look at the fruits of the Spirit and think in terms of all or nothing. Either we are patient or we are not. We are generous or we are not. Such extremes hardly fit the human situation, and certainly not with adolescents who are struggling with their identities and their place in the world.

Responding to the gifts of the Spirit does not mean that the fruits of the Spirit are simply going to be evidenced in us. Rather, it means that there will be evidence that we are growing in these qualities, becoming more like Christ all the time.

Teenagers know instinctively about becoming (growing) because they're in the constant process of doing it. It would be both fun and instructive to pull out old photo albums and do some remembering. It will be a great reminder that physically, emotionally, socially, they're not the same persons they were a year earlier. In the same way, spiritually we are also in an ongoing journey.

There are some practical ways we can discern and measure how we are growing in the life of the Spirit.

For discussion: Take each of the seven gifts of the Holy Spirit and, as a family, choose the gift that is most wanted. Why is that gift so important?

Simulated Conversation: Do I Have Any Choice?

The two simulated conversations in this chapter are meant to provide encouragement, increase the comfort level, and spark the imagination of parents in discussing Confirmation and related issues with their teenage children.

Dad: What are you reading?

Sam: Oh, this thing Mr. Elliot gave us for Confirmation class.

Dad: Homework for Confirmation class? I'm impressed.

Sam: Not usually. This is just an article to help us with some questions we might have. We're supposed to write down any questions and bring them to class.

Dad: What do you have down?

Sam: Nothing.

Dad: You understand it all?

Sam: No, I guess not. But I really don't know how to ask about what confuses me.

Dad: For example. . .

Sam: Well, this article says we're all going to receive the Holy Spirit. But not every person in our class goes to Church and lives the way Christians are supposed to. Yesterday, Tony told me that he

doesn't even really believe in all this Holy Spirit stuff.

Dad: Why is Tony being confirmed?

Sam: Because his parents are making him.

Dad: Why are you being confirmed?

Sam: Because that's what you're supposed to do when you're my age.

Dad: So nobody's giving you a choice about it?

Sam: No.

Dad: Hmmm. . . . When you were baptized, your mother and I and your godparents made promises to God for you. Why didn't you just walk in and commit yourself to the Church on your own?

Sam: Dad, please. I was just a baby!

Dad: That's right. You couldn't

even crawl, and didn't know the first thing about the Church. But that's not the case anymore. You really hate it when your mother and I make decisions for you now.

Sam: Because I'm old enough to make them myself.

Dad: You and Tony and every other kid in your class need to decide for yourselves if you want a personal relationship with God. When you were little we made choices for you. Hopefully, the values with which you've been raised will help you to make your own decision to be confirmed.

Sam: What do these decisions have to do with the Holy Spirit?

Dad: In Confirmation, the Spirit invites you to make a courageous commitment to always live as a good Christian. The call comes from the Holy Spirit. You are invited to make a free response and choice. God has never forced himself on any person yet. Ask Tony. God loves us so much that He gave us the freedom to choose whether or not we want to love Him back. As an adult, you can now make an informed decision and deal with the consequences that come from it.

Sam: Well, in that case, I've decided to move my curfew to four in the morning and to take the car out whenever I want. . . .

Dad: I don't think so. . . . You may be an adult in the eyes of the Church, young man, but you'd never survive that decision.

What Would It Be Like to Know the Lord Personally?

One way we can discern and measure how we are growing in the life of the Spirit is in our prayer life. We can think of prayer as the reciting of words either spontaneously or by formula. That is a component of prayer. But that describes a way that we do it, not what it is. Prayer is communication, and through communication a relationship with the Lord.

One of the many cries of parents to teenagers — "Talk to me!" — has a corollary in one of the many cries of teenagers to parents — "Listen to me!" Both say: Communicate! It is true that parents may not like what they hear and young people may not like how the parents respond after listening, still the fact doesn't dampen the need and desire to communicate. Now obviously if there isn't any talking and listening going on in a family, there isn't going to be much of a relationship. The desire to hear and be heard is, on a deeper level, a desire for relationship. That, too, is the way it is with prayer. We desire a relationship with the Lord.

Four understandings of prayer have evolved in the Catholic tradition: prayer as praise (or adoration), thanksgiving, contrition, petition.

- Petition, the prayer of "asking for," is the most commonly used.

- In contrition, we express sorrow and ask for forgiveness.

- In thanksgiving, we express gratitude for blessings we have received.

- In praise, we express love for the Lord and exalt His qualities.

These are not artificial distinctions, but forms of communication with parallels in human experience. In the relationships of family and friendships, we ask for help, comfort, guidance, companionship, support, etc.

When we have offended someone, we say — "I'm sorry." "Please forgive me." "Can we be friends again?" Or the all-teenage question: "Am I grounded?"

When a kindness or a favor has been done, we say — "Thanks!" "I appreciate it!" "You shouldn't have."

When we care about someone, we say — "You're terrific!" "You're the most wonderful person I know." And, of course, the immortal words, "I love you."

And when these communications happen, relationships are enriched and more intimately bonded.

It works the same way with the Lord. By speaking to the Lord similarly, our relationship with Him is enriched and more intimately bonded. And that is why we pray.

For discussion: With your son or daughter, or with your whole family, each working individually, write down how you believe you are good talkers and listeners and how you could do better at each. Share your thoughts with each other. In addition to working out better ways of communicating with each other, discuss what the shared reflections show about how we could better communicate with God.

Is It Time for an Attitude Assessment?

Another way we can discern and measure growth in our life in the Spirit is by how our attitudes are changing — attitudes about others, about ourselves, and about life in general. Teens are very sensitive to how they are treated. They are vulnerable to attitudes of others, oftentimes judged by the vibes they get rather than from specific actions.

When talking about attitudes, we're touching upon character — not what we do, but who we are. One way we can see evidence of growth in this area is by the fruits of the Holy Spirit mentioned above. Another measure we can use is from the famous passage on Christian love in 1 Corinthians, chapter 13. We can have faith to move mountains or give away everything we own, but if we don't have love, it counts for nothing.

So we can encourage our teenagers to ask themselves whether they are growing in the qualities of Christian love, as described by St. Paul.

- **Patience.** Am I willing to give others the time and space they need, or do I react hastily when I don't get my way or when others "get in my way"?

- **Kindness.** Am I sympathetic to the needs of others and considerate of their feelings, or do I extend myself to others only when I have to?

- **Not jealous.** Do the achievements and gains of others make me happy, or do I resent others because of their successes or because of what they have?

- **Not pompous** (doesn't put on airs). Am I honest about who I am, or do I put on an act or fabricate stories to impress others?

- **Not inflated** (snobbish). Do I recognize others for their qualities and as equals in the eyes of God, or do I put others down by acting superior to them and look down on those who have less than I?

- **Not rude.** Do I encourage others, or do I say things to humiliate others and treat others as if they don't count?

- **Not self-seeking.** Do I put the needs of others before mine and am I generous in giving my time and talents, or do I think only about "what's in it for me?"

- **Not quick-tempered.** Am I calm when I don't get my way, or do I throw a fit and look for ways of getting back at others?

- **Does not brood over injury.** When wronged by someone, do I face the situation and try to seek reconciliation, or do I whine and sulk?

- **Does not rejoice over wrongdoing but rejoices with the truth.** Do I find joy in the kind, fair, and just treatment of others, or do I revel in gossip and slander and in seeing others put down?

For discussion: Have participants add their own questions following the quality listed. Have each person fill in a "temperature rating" for each of the ten qualities. You might want to use the following guidelines for each quality: 10 — on fire; 9 — hot; 8 — warm; 7 — lukewarm; 6 — mild; 5 — cool; 4 — chilly; 3 — crisp; 2 — cold; 1 — frigid; 0 — frozen. Add each of the ten ratings to the thermometer. What is the total temperature? What are some ways your teenager and other participants can increase their temperatures? How can we grow in the qualities of Christian love?

Simulated Conversation: How Will I Be Different?

Debbie: I can't believe you couch potatoes are just sitting there in front of the TV.

Mom: Excuse me? Is this our watch-a-holic daughter preaching?

Debbie: I'm serious, Mom. You should have heard Father talking to our Confirmation class. There's so much to be done. Unborn babies to be saved, hungry people to feed. We're not doing a thing.

Dad: Speak for yourself!

Debbie: Sure, you volunteer for all sorts of things, but is what you're doing really making any difference?

Dad: Would you like to talk about this or just yell at us?

Debbie: Well, I was thinking about how after Pentecost the apostles had all this courage to go around preaching to people. Most of them were killed because of it. I'm going to be confirmed, but what's going to happen? I'll probably be the same old me.

Mom: Oh? Maybe you need to *expect* to be different, to *want* to be different.

Dad: Perhaps you have the idea that there will be some sort of dramatic and instantaneous transformation at Confirmation.

Debbie: Well, if Confirmation is so important, why not?

Dad: Receiving the Holy Spirit is no magic act. The Holy Spirit lovingly calls you to the Sacrament of Confirmation. Your free decision to respond is a big one, but it is just the first of many decisions which show that you are open to the Holy Spirit's action in your life.

Debbie: Uh oh. I don't like the sound of this.

Dad: Nobody said that being a Christian is easy. It would be nice if we could be instantaneously holy. Poof! But that's not the way it works.

Debbie: Then how will I be different? How will the Holy Spirit be at work in my life?

Dad: Well, you seem to be concerned about unborn babies and hungry people. Aren't you?

Debbie: Yes.

Dad: Okay, that's a sign you're growing in your faith. There's hope for you yet.

Mom: Don't tease. This is important. Debbie, you're not going to be able to effectively reach out to the needy unless you have respect for them.

Debbie: Whom don't I respect?

Mom: Don't be defensive. I'm just recalling some conversations I've overheard in which you and your friends were laughing about some girls in your school who weren't "with it."

Debbie: I told them they were being mean.

Mom: Okay, think of how awful you'd feel if you served at a soup kitchen and saw one of those girls with her family there.

Debbie: I'd die!

Dad: You wouldn't be so embarrassed if you care for people as they are and treat them as you would want to be treated.

Debbie: So what are you saying?

Dad: It shows you're growing in the Spirit when you grow in respect for people, especially those less fortunate than yourself.

Debbie: All right. I'll try to shape up my friends and be more sensitive to others, if you can tell me how your volunteer stuff does the world any good.

Mom: It's a deal!

Actions Speak Louder Than Words

A third way that our life in the Spirit can be discerned and measured is in our willingness to act upon our faith and the determination to follow through with service to others. It follows from Jesus' new commandment: "Love one another. As I have loved you, so you also should love one another" (John 13:34). It may sound like a command for the Mother Teresas of the world, but it is for every Catholic who has received the Spirit through the Sacraments of Baptism and Confirmation. Jesus continues to say: "This is how all will know that you are my disciples, if you have love for one another" (v. 35).

Service is the "put your money where your mouth is" part of our faith. When we say in the creed, "We believe in God. . . . We believe in Jesus Christ. . . . We believe in the Holy Spirit. . . . We believe in the Catholic Church," a voice (conscience? the Spirit within us?) says, "show me!" It is shown through service to others and self-sacrificing love.

The desire to serve in teenagers can be discerned in small things. They need not be headline-grabbing projects, and in fact almost always are not. It may involve reaching out to a family member beyond established family duties, something as small as doing the dishes out of turn. It may involve giving up going to a friend's house to help a younger brother or sister with homework. It may involve participating in a parish outreach to a soup kitchen, a homeless shelter, or home for unwed mothers. It may involve befriending a student in school who is ignored or snubbed by peers. It may involve standing up for our faith when its values are being attacked rather than being passive and shrugging as if the attack was no big deal. It may involve helping a neighbor with shoveling snow or raking leaves, or visiting a shut-in and talking and listening with the person, or doing some free baby-sitting for a single mother who just lost her job and desperately needs a break.

The list is endless and deciding on appropriate actions requires nothing more than the will to do it and perhaps a little inquiring.

For discussion: What actions show that the Spirit is alive in me? What could I further do that would illustrate my willingness to grow in the Spirit? (Suggestion: Again, try to do this as a shared activity. A parent's witness is the most convincing reason for a child to become a witness.)

What the Church Says About Confirmation

Confirmation is the strengthening and fullness of the Holy Spirit received already in Baptism. Confirmation, together with Baptism and Eucharist, are known as the Sacraments of Christian Initiation and therefore are a unity.

Confirmation calls us to a greater participation in the mission of Jesus and the Church. The grace of this sacrament challenges us to be "like" Christ in all we do and say.

Through Confirmation our relationship with God is deepened and we are incorporated more completely into the body of Christ. Confirmation obliges us, as true witnesses of Christ, to spread and defend the faith by word and deed.

Confirmation, like Baptism, imprints a spiritual mark on the soul. Thus, Confirmation is only received once.

In the celebration of the sacrament, the bishop extends his hands over all those to be confirmed and invokes the outpouring of the Holy Spirit. Sacred chrism is used for anointing. The conferring of the Sacrament of Confirmation is done through the anointing with chrism on the forehead, the laying on of hands, and through the words, "Be sealed with the gift of the Holy Spirit."

The sign of peace which concludes the sacrament reveals and expresses ecclesial communion with the bishop and all the faithful.

The bishop is the ordinary minister of Confirmation. It is appropriate from the very meaning of the sacrament, that he should confer it himself. For this very reason, Confirmation has been separated from Baptism. Because Confirmation invites those who receive it more closely to the Church, and missions them to bear witness to Christ, it is appropriate that it be given by one who has received the fullness of the Sacrament of Orders.

Mary

Cindy Cavnar

Mary: Who Needs Her?

Times have changed. Not too long ago, it was extremely difficult for parents to talk to their children about sex. After a hasty exposition of the facts, most parents lapsed into confused silence. Many kids were lucky to get even that. Today our children are more savvy. Many have been exposed to sex education in their schools, and with all the attention given on TV or in school to AIDS, abortion, sexual harassment, and homosexuality, most kids are just "aware."

So, attention to sex has become open and pervasive. Interestingly, about the same time attention to sex became open and pervasive, Mary, the mother of Jesus, became enshrouded under a veil of secrecy. It used to be easy for parents to talk to their children about Mary. May processions, the rosary, and popular devotions gave her a high profile in Catholic life.

Following the Second Vatican Council, many of those Marian devotions fell to the wayside. With them fell a sense of certainty about who Mary is for Christians today. As parents, we often approach the topic with the same trepidation we once reserved for sex education. If we mention Mary to our children at all, it is to present a brief exposition of the facts. Or to pray a decade of the rosary. Then, silence.

Frankly, many of us are confused, and with good reason. The issue of Marian devotion evokes widely divergent viewpoints. Some feminist Christians, for example, reject Mary as too passive and submissive. Other feminists, in revolt against what they perceive as a male-dominated religion, have exalted Mary into a kind of goddess.

On the other hand, some well-meaning Catholics have gone over the edge in the extravagance of their devotion to Mary. Others have virtually dismissed her in a misguided attempt at ecumenical sensitivity.

And then there is the average person, who hasn't given Mary much thought at all.

Who *is* Mary for Christians today? Is there a reasonable approach to the issue? Catholics have long regarded her as a powerful intercessor. We also honor her as the mother of the Savior. Beyond that, we're often at a loss. Why? In large part because she frequently seems remote and inaccessible.

A Few Words Say Much

Mary is recorded only seven times in the Scriptures, but her few words point out much about her faith, strength, joy, concern, and care. What do these passages signify?

" 'How can this be, since I have no relations with a man?' "
— Luke 1:34

" 'Behold, I am the handmaid of the Lord. May it be done to me according to your word.' "
— Luke 1:38

"[Mary] entered the house of Zechariah and greeted Elizabeth."
— Luke 1:40

" 'My soul proclaims the greatness of the Lord.' "
— Luke 1:46-55

" 'Son, why have you done this to us? Your father and I have been looking for you with great anxiety.' "
Luke 2:38

" 'They have no wine.' "
— John 2:3

" 'Do whatever he tells you.' "
— John 2:5

We exalt her as Queen of Heaven but fail to see her as the hardworking Jewish peasant that she was. St. Thérèse of Lisieux, commenting on this point, said that she never heard a sermon about Mary that she liked. Some people, she said, would feel "a certain estrangement from a creature so superior."[*] This indeed seems to be the case.

If your children are to develop a lasting relationship with Mary, they need to get to know her as friend, confidant, and mother. They don't need to know her as an austere heavenly creature.

The same is true for you, if you expect to lead them into that relationship. Before you talk to your children, address your own concerns. If you appear hesitant and uncertain, your kids will disregard what you say.

Take a couple of weeks to pray about Mary and her role in Jesus' life before you tackle the subject with your children. Reflect on scriptural references to her. Ask the Lord to guide you to a correct appreciation of His mother.

For reflection: Who is Mary to you?

*See _Story of a Soul: The Autobiography of St. Thérèse of Lisieux._

You've Got a Friend

If you're trying to grab children's attention, nothing works like the story of a miracle. Physical healings are particularly impressive. In fact, the more repulsive the physical condition prior to the healing, the more attentive your audience will be. Nothing like a graphic story to stimulate young minds.

That's what I used to think. Not too long ago I had an experience with my kids that taught me otherwise. I had just finished reading *The Miracle of Lourdes*[*] by Ruth Cranston, a fascinating account of many of the miracles that have taken place through Mary's intercession at Lourdes.

At that point in our family, we had not spoken of Mary for some time. I was convinced these stories would get us back on track. I picked the particularly vivid case of Gabriel Gargam, a railway worker nearly crushed to death in a train accident. Gargam suffered terribly for two years before his instantaneous cure at Lourdes during the procession of the Blessed Sacrament. One minute he was paralyzed, the next he was on his feet trying to follow the procession.

I sat our kids down to listen. At fourteen, thirteen, and ten, they were the perfect ages for this approach. Or so I thought. I read the story and looked up to bored, blank faces. I read another. Same response. I gave up.

Shortly after, I discovered another book, *The Miraculous Medal*[**] by Mary Fabyan Windeatt. This book, aimed at seven- to twelve-year-olds, tells the story of Mary's appearances to Catherine Labouré. I read it to our ten-year-old Tim within earshot of the others. This time, I got a very positive response.

What was the difference? Both books are excellent and highly recommended. The problem lay with the way I approached the material. Children are not attracted to a God who pops in now and then to bestow a spectacular miracle. What they're really looking for, although they may not be able to articulate it, is a relationship. This is especially true of pre-teens and teens.

In the story of Catherine Labouré, they heard about a very ordinary woman and her relationship with God and Mary. True, she had extraordinary experiences, but those took place within the context of her everyday life. I hadn't ripped the story out of its setting, as I had done with

---

[*]Ruth Cranston, *Miracle of Lourdes* (New York: Doubleday, 1988).

[**]Mary F. Windeatt, *The Miraculous Medal* (Rockford, Ill.: TAN Bks Pubs.).

the Gargam healing. Through Catherine's life, the kids could see that God and Mary are interested in an on-going relationship, not guest appearances.

What does this mean for us as we try to talk with our children about Jesus' mother?

Obviously, we want to emphasize the fact that there is the potential here for a wonderful friendship between Mary and the child. This is relatively easy to do with very young children. They have a concrete, uncomplicated experience of human love. Mom and Dad love them and they, in turn, love Mom and Dad.

A series of appropriate questions might get the ball rolling. You might ask your four-year-old what she thinks Jesus liked best about bedtime at His house. Was it the bedtime stories His mother told Him? Was it the prayers His mom and dad prayed with Him? Was it the way His mother tucked Him into bed?

You want your child to understand that Mary was a warm, friendly, loving mom, a lot like your child's own mom. Emphasize that Mary loves each of us just as she loved Jesus. She wants to be our mother and friend.

You can use the same approach, on a more grown-up level, with children through the age of ten or so.

Teenagers, on the other hand, may not feel particularly warm toward Mom and Dad. Any attempt to link Mary to their own parents is apt to backfire. Further, most pre-teens and teens are not openly interested in a relationship with Mary. Some of them have never thought of it. Others think they want nothing to do with Mary because, as one teenager told me, she was "too perfect." How could she possibly understand their struggles and fears?

Let's take a deeper look at a potential stumbling block for your children and their relationship with the mother of Jesus.

For reflection: Are you comfortable in helping your children develop a relationship with Mary? Why or why not?

Mary: Perfectly Ordinary

If your children protest that Mary was "too perfect," they probably don't mean simply that she was free from original sin (the doctrine of the Immaculate Conception). They have a looser definition in mind. To kids, perfect might mean overly-refined, remote, or unaggressive. A perfect person is a do-gooder, teacher's pet, humor-impaired. All the things your child doesn't want to be.

And all the things, we can be sure, that Mary never was. She wasn't a remote figure devoid of emotion. She was a real human being who faced life head-on, grappled with it, and forged ahead. Every day. Day in, day out.

This requires enormous strength and courage, traits your kids might not associate with Mary. It also requires the grace of God, which they will associate with Mary but probably as a passive characteristic. Most likely, they will not imagine that she ever had to seize that grace and cling to it in the face of strong emotion.

But she did. Ask your kids to think about a time they felt rejected. Did Mary ever feel that way? How about the time shortly after she conceived Jesus? Scripture tells us that Joseph decided to divorce her, the ultimate rejection for a woman of her time.

How did Mary feel? Confused? Lonely? Isn't that how we all feel when we're rejected? Isn't it possible, you might ask your children, that Mary does understand how they feel at those moments?

Have your children ever been afraid? Maybe they've been lost. Maybe they've been seriously ill. Maybe they've only had to endure a tyrannical teacher. Mary can identify with their fear. Do they know that a woman in her position — pregnant, unmarried, engaged — faced the possibility of death by stoning? How do they think Mary felt?

What do they know about daily life in ancient Israel? Mary was a poor woman who worked at a pitch few of us can imagine. Under the influence of overly-pious Marian images, your children may have placed her in solitary splendor on a jeweled throne. If you want to position her in the rough and tumble of ordinary life, take a look at *Daily Life in the Time of Jesus*[*] by Henri Daniel-Rops. It will give you the facts you need to paint a more realistic picture of Mary's world.

---

[*]Henri Daniel-Rops, tr. by Patrick O'Brian, *Daily Life in the Time of Jesus* (Ann Arbor, Mich.: Servant Pubns., 1981).

Mary: The Perfect Prayer Partner[**] will also help your children enter into Mary's life. This book, by Father Kenneth Roberts, combines an introduction to Mary with brief meditations on the mysteries of the rosary. Without descending into sentimentality, Father Roberts concentrates on Mary's feelings as she met various events in her life. He does the same with Jesus.

Don't *give* this book to your children; *use* it with them. Try praying a decade of the rosary together. Read aloud the meditations for that mystery. Don't force a discussion of the material. If the kids want to comment, they will.

Your goal, as you talk and pray with your kids, is simple. You want to dismantle any notion your children might have that Mary, in her perfection, is distant and unapproachable. Yes, she was free from sin. But she was also, in many ways, ordinary. Perfectly ordinary and perfectly accessible to your kids at every stage of development.

For reflection: Think about how Mary probably felt during her experiences related above. Consider also how she felt when she realized that Jesus, at the age of twelve, was "lost" as she and Joseph were returning from the Passover and they returned to Jerusalem to find Him. Imagine her feelings as Jesus met resistance from some of the Jewish leaders. Consider her pain in witnessing her Son's suffering and death. Do you feel she can understand your feelings?

[**]Kenneth Roberts, Fr., *Mary: The Perfect Prayer Partner* (Huntington, Ind.: Our Sunday Visitor, 1990).

Simulated Conversation: Jesus Out on the Town

The two simulated conversations in this chapter are meant to provide encouragement, increase the comfort level, and spark the imagination of parents in discussing Mary with their children.

A conversation between a parent and an intermediate grade child . . .

Dad: Hey, Bill, remember I told you to listen carefully to the Gospel every Sunday? I want to talk about it after Mass each week.

Bill: Sure, Dad.

Dad: Well, what did you think?

Bill: What did I think about what?

Dad: Today's Gospel. C'mon. Stop playing games with me.

Bill: I wondered how Jesus got away with it.

Dad: Got away with what?

Bill: Hanging around in Jerusalem after His parents left. First, He gets Himself lost for three days and then He tells His mom and dad they shouldn't have bothered looking for Him. Boy, talk about trouble. You guys would've nailed me.

Dad: Maybe we would have. But there's something deeper going on here. Didn't Father's sermon help you understand the story?

Bill: You just said I had to listen to the Gospel. You didn't say anything about the sermon.

Dad: Oh, brother. Well, believe it or not, the Gospel isn't about how Jesus managed to sneak around Jerusalem. It's really about the fact that He was growing up and becoming more aware of the job He was sent to do.

Bill: That's not as exciting.

Dad: Actually, it's very exciting.

Bill: I'll bet Joseph and Mary didn't think so.

Dad: What do you mean?

Bill: Sometimes Mom tells me how much she'll miss me when I grow up and move away. I'll bet Mary was sad to think that Jesus was already thinking of leaving home. He was only twelve!

Dad: You know, that's a good point. I think Mary was sad and scared and even a little bit angry. When they found Jesus, she didn't just ask Him where he had been. She said, "Why did you do this to us?" It's like she couldn't believe that He would hurt them so deliberately.

Bill: That sounds like Mom, except she would start hollering. Mary didn't holler.

Dad: Maybe she was thinking things over. Remember, she knew Jesus was special. The angel had told her that when he announced Jesus' birth. And then the holy man, Simeon, told her that her son could be responsible for the downfall of a lot of people and the rise of others. She knew Jesus was different, but I don't think she knew exactly what that meant.

Bill: So you mean that when Jesus stuck around in Jerusalem, it was just another weird thing she couldn't figure out?

Dad: Well, I wouldn't call it weird. Let's just say it was one more piece of the puzzle. The Gospel tells us that Jesus returned to Nazareth with His family and Mary "kept all these things in her heart."

Bill: That must have been hard.

Dad: I think it was. She had to have a lot of trust in God. Life wasn't easy for her, wondering what was going to become of her son. She handled all the years of waiting and wondering and anxiety, moments like losing Jesus in Jerusalem, by trusting in God.

Bill: Well, that's kind of different from what I got out of the story.

Dad: You're telling me. How about next week we read the Gospel before we go to church. Maybe that'll help. Oh, and Bill . . . pay attention to the sermon.

Feast Days: Oh, No!
Is This a Holy Day of Obligation?

It's 11 p.m. and you're exhausted. You have one thought on your mind — sleep. Suddenly, unbidden, another thought swims into your head. Feast day. Could it be? Is tomorrow really the feast of the Assumption? Yes, you're sure of it. But wait a minute. It's on a Saturday this year. Didn't the bishop excuse the diocese from attending the feast-day Mass? Or did he?

Confused, you drift into sleep. In the morning you'll track down the Mass schedule, rearrange activities, and get everyone off to church.

Welcome to another meaningful Marian feast.

Contrary to popular belief, the Church didn't institute holy days in order to disrupt family life. For centuries, in the context of the Mass, they served as an opportunity for teaching on specific areas of the faith. Plus, they were occasions for celebrations in the village, town, or nation. Prayer time and party time.

These days, you're not likely to rally the family for a procession in Mary's honor. Still, feast days provide natural opportunities to take a deeper look at Mary and her role in the Church.

There are only three holy days of obligation associated with Mary (see "Some Feast Days of Mary," p. 104). There's no need to limit yourselves to those. Use the feasts associated with Mary's apparitions (more about them on p. 106).

Or consider, for example, the feast of the Annunciation. "We already know that story," your kids will say. True, but have they considered it from a contemporary angle?

Here's what Malcolm Muggeridge has to say about the Annunciation in his book *Jesus.*[*] A modern woman would regard the message Mary received from the Angel Gabriel as "ill-tidings of great sorrow and a slur on the local family-planning center. . . . Mary's pregnancy, in poor circumstances, and with the father unknown, would have been an obvious case for an abortion; and her talk of having conceived as a result of the intervention of the Holy Ghost would have pointed to the need for psychiatric treatment, and made the case for terminating her pregnancy even stronger."

This approach could prompt some questions, geared to the ages of your children. What does Mary's response to the angel say about her strength of character? What does it say about her confidence in God? What do your kids think of Mary's surprise pregnancy in the light of today's abortion mentality?

You don't need to limit feast days to discussion. A special meal is always in order. If you have young children, have a party complete with birthday cake on September 8, the feast of the birth of Mary.

---

[*]Malcolm Muggeridge, *Jesus* (San Francisco: HarperCollins, 1976).

Some Feast Days of Mary

Holy Days of Obligation

January 1	Solemnity of Mary, Mother of God
August 15	The Assumption
December 8	The Immaculate Conception

General Feast Days

February 11	Our Lady of Lourdes
March 25	The Annuniciation
May 31	The Visitation
July 16	Our Lady of Mt. Carmel
August 22	The Queenship of Mary
September 15	Mary, Mother of Sorrows
October 7	Our Lady of the Rosary
December 12	Our Lady of Guadalupe

Close out your meal or discussion with a brief, simple prayer. Have everyone mention something about Mary that they like or that impresses them. Or have them each ask Mary to intercede for a personal need. Read an appropriate passage from Scripture and end with a Hail Mary or a spontaneous prayer.

Try to work four or five Marian feasts into your calendar each year. These would be occasions in which you talk about Mary as well as have a party or go to Mass. That may not seem like much, but over the years it will establish a rhythm in your family life. The kids will pick up facts about Mary but also the sense that she is a dynamic presence, relevant even today.

***

For discussion: What are ways you can make Marian feast days a more important part of your family life?

Simulated Conversation: Was Mary Bossy?

A conversation between a parent and a junior high child . . .

Mom: Why so glum, Emily?

Emily: I have to read the Gospel for next Sunday's Mass and write what I think it means. It's a pain.

Mom: Are you having trouble understanding it?

Emily: Nope. I understand it, but it bothers me.

Mom: Why don't you tell me about it?

Emily: The Gospel is the story of the wedding feast at Cana.

Mom: Don't you like the story?

Emily: Parts of it. I mean, it's neat when Jesus turns the water into wine. I'll bet the steward freaked out. But I think Mary was kind of bossy.

Mom: In what way?

Emily: Well, first she tells Jesus the wine has run out. He says, "So what?" Obviously, He doesn't want to do anything about it. Does Mary drop it? No way. She goes and tells the servants to do whatever Jesus tells them to do. If you ask me, that's bossy and kind of sneaky, too.

Mom: Hmm, I get your point. But maybe there's another way of looking at this. For example, maybe Mary told Jesus about the wine because she felt sorry for the bride and groom. She could imagine how embarrassed they felt.

Emily: I still think she was nagging Jesus.

Mom: I doubt it. She wanted the couple to be happy on their wedding day. It shows how alert Mary was to the needs of those around her.

Emily: But what about the way she ignores Jesus and tells everybody to go ahead and obey Him?

Mom: Actually, Emily, this is my favorite part of the story. For me, it says that Mary was so close to Jesus that she could ask Him anything. She knew that Jesus would answer her. She wasn't afraid of approaching Him and He wanted very much to respond to her. They must have loved each other a lot.

Emily: I like that. Okay. So she wasn't nagging Him and she wasn't bossy.

Mom: But there's more, Emily. Mary's heart went out to that couple and she didn't hesitate to go to Jesus on their behalf. That's what she does for us, too.

Emily: You mean, she'll go to Jesus for me?

Mom: Sure. She wants you to talk to Jesus yourself, but she also wants you to talk to her. She'll bring your prayers before the Lord. You can see how powerful her intercession was at Cana. Well, it's just as powerful for you.

Emily: That sounds good, but I'll have to think about that, Mom.

Mom: That sounds good to me.

Marian Apparitions

Recently I talked to my son, Tim, about Mary's appearances to people in the twentieth century. You have to be careful about these claims, I told him. Sometimes people think they see her when, in fact, they don't. "I know what you mean," he said. "Like people who think they see her face in the leftovers in the refrigerator."

That was not quite what I had in mind, but I thought Tim had the general idea. He wasn't being disrespectful; he was simply reflecting the sort of oddball story he had heard on the news.

The Church is very cautious about accepting Marian apparitions. Even when it does give its approval, as in the appearances at Lourdes, the Church does not require us to accept the story or subsequent miracles. Actions speak louder than words, however. Many popes have been deeply moved by accounts of various apparitions.

Pope John Paul II, for example, was gunned down in an assassination attempt on May 13, 1981. This was the anniversary of Mary's first appearance at Fátima. A year to the day later, convinced that Mary had protected him, he made a pilgrimage of thanksgiving to Fátima.

The stories of Mary's appearances are electrifying. Your kids need to hear them. Even a jaded TV generation will recognize that these are something special.

For preschoolers, your best bet would be to read a particular story yourself and then tell it in your own words. Both *Cause of Our Joy,*[*] by Sister Mary Francis Le Blanc, and *Those Who Saw Her*[**] by Catherine Odell recount the stories of many Marian apparitions.

There is plenty of other material available on the topic. Don't miss the excellent comic books about Our Lady of Guadalupe published by Franciscan Communications. Special mention should also be given the new Emmy award winning film, "Fátima." Using footage of actual historic events, the movie weaves the wars and unrest of the twentieth century into the context of the Fátima story. It is appropriate for a teenage or adult audience.

When discussing any of the Marian apparitions with your children, be sure to emphasize her message. Usually, this will have something to do with prayer and penance.

At Fátima, for example, Mary specifically linked the possibility of peace to the necessity of prayer and penance. Today, even very young children are concerned about the threat of war. They feel helpless and frightened. Ask them what Mary has to say about peace. Is it simply a concern of politicians or does it have something to do with the way ordinary people live their lives? If the latter is true, what can they do to foster peace? What does it mean to make sacrifices or do penance for peace? Why is Mary concerned about this issue?

Mary appeared to two children at La Sallette, France in 1846. Among other things, she told them that the local men should stop swearing. What a contemporary message! Why would Mary be concerned about their language? What do your children think? Ask your children what their language says about their interior state. Do they swear? How can they stop? Why should they stop?

All the Marian apparitions offer extensive opportunity for discussion and reflection. Tell the stories of these appearances on the appropriate feast days or tell them at any time of the year. But do tell them. They can be one of your most effective means for introducing your children to Mary.

Mary has achieved what we all hope to achieve: She is with God, body and soul, in heaven. This is good news, better than we might think. Why?

---

[*]M. Francis Le Blanc, Sr., *Cause of Our Joy* (Boston: Daughters of St. Paul, 1981).

[**]Catherine Odell, *Those Who Saw Her* (Huntington, Ind.: Our Sunday Visitor, 1986).

Because she hasn't forgotten us. As our friend, confidant, intercessor, mother, and model of holiness, she is ready to accompany us as we journey toward God.

St. Francis de Sales once said, "Our Lady comes to visit us very often but we do not really want to receive her." Let's not make that mistake. We need her and our children need her. If we welcome her, she will stand with us and lead us to her Son.

For reflection: What will it take to have greater peace in the world? In your family? In your personal life? What role does prayer and penance play in attaining peace?

What the Church Says About Mary

What the Catholic faith believes about Mary is founded upon what it believes about Christ. What it teaches about Mary illuminates in turn the Church's faith in Christ.

The Annunciation ushered in the fullness of time, the time of fulfillment of God's promises and preparation for the coming of the Messiah. The Holy Spirit, the Lord and giver of Life, was sent to sanctify Mary's virginal womb and make it divinely fruitful, causing her to conceive the eternal Son, Christ, with a human nature derived from her own.

From all eternity, God chose as His Son's mother a daughter of Israel, Mary, a young Jewish woman of Nazareth in Galilee. Through the centuries, the Church believes that from the moment of her conception, Mary was filled with grace by God. This is the dogma of the Immaculate Conception proclaimed by Pope Pius IX in 1854.

Mary gave her consent to God's Word and embraced His saving plan with all her heart and, without a single sin to restrain her, Mary, the mother of Jesus, gave herself entirely to her Son's person and work, with Him, dependent on Him, and by God's grace, to serve the mystery of redemption. Mary was acclaimed by Elizabeth, under the impulse of the Spirit and even before the birth of her Son, as "the mother of my Lord."

The Church has always confessed that Jesus was conceived by the power of the Holy Spirit alone, "without human seed, from the Holy Spirit." Christ's birth did not lessen Mary's virginal integrity but consecrated it. The

Church celebrates Mary as "Ever-virgin." Jesus is Mary's only son, but her spiritual motherhood extends to all whom Jesus came to save.

Faith, in the context of the whole of revelation, discovers the mysterious reasons why God's saving plan wanted His Son to be born of a virgin.

Mary's virginity reveals God's absolute initiative in the incarnation.

Jesus was conceived by the Holy Spirit in the Virgin Mary's womb because He is the New Adam, who ushers in the new creation.

By His virginal conception, Jesus, the New Adam, ushered in the new birth of children adopted in the Holy Spirit through faith.

Mary's virginity is the sign of her unhesitating faith and undivided gift of herself to God's will.

Mary is the most perfect symbol and realization of the Church, who by faithfully accepting God's Word, becomes a mother, for by preaching and Baptism she brings forth children conceived by the Holy Spirit and born of God to new and immortal life. The Church is also a virgin who keeps integral and pure the faith pledged to her spouse.

Prayer

Mary Ann Kuharski

Alleluia From Head to Toe

How do we talk to our children about prayer? How do we teach them to pray? How do we let them know that God wants to be part of their everyday lives? These are common questions many Christian parents face.

St. Augustine was a great sinner who reformed and became one of the greatest saints of all time. He said that each one of us should be a walking "Alleluia from head to toe." Our lives should be examples of "Alleluia" to others. Our daily activity should be a prayer to God.

A walking "alleluia from head to toe!" sounds good in theory. But how does the average Christian couple get that across to their children — especially in today's fast-paced culture?

We can begin with the basics. We can teach our young the simple little prayers: the Our Father, the Hail Mary, the Glory Be. We can teach and use the Bless Us, O Lord, the prayer before meals. But there is much more we can do to teach youngsters about prayer.

My husband, John, and I are the parents of thirteen children, ages four to twenty-four. Seven of our children came by "tummy" — as the kids say — and six came by "airport" or adoption. All have given us an intangible gift that cannot be bought or stolen. They have brought their parents closer to God and to each other.

As we worked to bring our values and faith to our children, we learned something. No matter what the challenges of the day, and regardless of our culture, there was more goodness in our daily lives if prayer was there. Prayer is a must.

The Church teaches that God will give us all the grace and tools we need to guide our young. For us, helping our children to learn the value of prayer is one giant step forward in parenting.

That is what this chapter is about: Teaching children to pray.

For reflection: How have your children brought you closer to God? How has prayer been a part of your family life?

Common Catholic Prayers

Prayer Before Meals

Bless us, O Lord, and these your gifts, which we are about to receive from your bounty. Through Christ our Lord. Amen.

Our Father

Our Father, who art in heaven, hallowed be thy name; thy kingdom come; thy will be done on earth as it is in heaven. Give us this day our daily bread; and forgive us our trespasses as we forgive those who trespass against us; and lead us not into temptation, but deliver us from evil. Amen.

Hail Mary

Hail Mary, full of grace, the Lord is with you. Blessed are you among women and blessed is the fruit of your womb, Jesus. Holy Mary, Mother of God, pray for us sinners now and at the hour of our death. Amen.

Glory Be

Glory be to the Father, and to the Son, and to the Holy Spirit. As it was in the beginning, is now, and ever shall be, world without end. Amen.

Apostles' Creed

I believe in God, the Father Almighty, Creator of heaven and earth; and in Jesus Christ, His only Son, Our Lord: Who was conceived by the Holy Spirit, born of the Virgin Mary, suffered under Pontius Pilate, was crucified, died, and was buried. He descended into hell: the third day He arose again from the dead; He ascended into heaven, sits at the right hand of God, the Father Almighty; from thence He shall come to judge the living and the dead. I believe in the Holy Spirit, the holy Catholic Church, the communion of saints, the forgiveness of sins, the resurrection of the body, and life everlasting. Amen.

Parents Are the First Missionaries

Parents are the first missionaries to their children. This truth is a source of encouragement for us because we are still "in the midst of the mess."

Often, parents fail to see that they are the first and best teachers of their children. That is understandable when you are knee deep in diapers, dirty dishes, or discipline decisions. But Christian mothers and fathers are doing something far more influential and powerful than any leader in the secular world. We have the power to shape the world, for years — in fact, for generations — to come. Our children and their children will become the future leaders. And what a frightening world this will be if they don't know about prayer!

Here are some points which could guide you as "missionaries":

- Fathers should take the lead. Recent studies show that in the area of faith, it is the father who will have the greatest impact on the children. He will shape the religious practices they will carry with them to adulthood. The sons will imitate the father. Daughters will generally choose a spouse most like their dad.

This does not mean that a single mother, or a family in which the father is a non-believer, has an impossible task. It simply means the mother must double her efforts.

- Stand united in prayer. "United we stand, divided we fall." Whether it is in simple household rules or in passing along fundamental beliefs, a united front is crucial for parents. When spouses are of different religions, or if one partner is unchurched, the children must witness respect for the Catholic beliefs, even if there is no complete agreement about them.

- Be flexible about rules. You probably learned early on in your life as a parent to be flexible. You learned not to expect perfection from your child. Remember that there will be occasions when your prayer times are less than perfect. Be consoled with some other words of St. Augustine: "The mere intent to pray can be a form of prayer."

- Let your children see you pray. In just about everything, children will see what you are doing and will do the same. Children need to see their parents in play, in prayer, and in love. Actions do speak louder than words. We will only become that walking "head to toe" Alleluia with prayer and persistence.

It Pays to 'Hang in There'

The Gospels tell about persistence in prayer.

In Luke 11:5-8, Jesus tells of a man going at midnight to a friend for bread. The friend and his family are in bed and the house is locked up. Jesus says that if the friend won't accommodate the man out of friendship, he will do so because of his persistence.

In Luke 18:1-8, Jesus tells the parable of the persistent widow. A judge neither feared God nor respected any human being. A widow kept bothering him to render a decision in her favor against an adversary. The judge finally relented to get her off his back.

The point is that God will not be slow to respond to those who call to him day and night in prayer.

In Luke 11:9-13, Jesus says: "Ask and you will receive; seek and you will find; knock and the door will be opened to you." He asks what father would give his son a snake rather than a fish, or a scorpion rather than an egg. Imagine then how God will give good gifts to those who ask.

Prayer in your family is vital to your role as the first missionaries to your children. If prayer has not previously been a part of your routine, tell your children that you now see that it will help your family. Ask your children to help you make prayer a rich and growing conversation. Let them have input concerning how you are going to pray as a family. The simple wisdom of children can be delightfully surprising.

For reflection: Make a list of all the things your children see you do. Which do you think have the most positive impact? Are there any things which might have a negative impact?

Simulated Conversation: Talking to God Really Is Prayer

The two simulated conversations in this chapter are meant to provide encouragement, increase the comfort level, and spark the imagination of parents in discussing prayer with their children.

An after-prayers-at-bedtime conversation between a parent and a young child . . .

Mom: Kari, we often talk to God just before you go to bed. Did you know that you can talk to God anytime you want?

Kari: I can? How?

Mom: Well, we all just prayed when we said our night prayers. We also fold our hands and pray before we eat. And we pray before we go to bed, or when we go to Mass. Those are times when we're talking to God. Prayer is talking to God.

Kari: Are there other times, too?

Mom: Sure. There are special prayers we say during Lent and Advent, or at Christmas and Easter time. Or we can talk to God at special times, like at the baby's Baptism.

Kari: Remember when we all prayed during the storm at Grandma's? That was scary!

Mom: Yes. We all felt better after we lit that candle and said a prayer.

Kari: I get it! Sometimes we pray when we're happy, sometimes when we're sad, and sometimes we pray because we're scared.

Mom: Right. And, of course, we pray when we're thankful — not just for food, but for all the gifts God gives us. But there's still other times when we can talk to God.

Kari: You mean like the time Angela went to the hospital in an ambulance?

Mom: That's right. Angie needed an operation to remove her appendix. She prayed and everyone at home prayed, too. All of us were talking to God and asking Him to guide the nurses and doctors helping Angela. God loves each of us so very much. He's just waiting for us to talk to Him. In fact, each time we pray, we're letting God know that we need Him and love Him.

Kari: What do I tell God?

Mom: Sometimes, you might pray the Our Father, Hail Mary, or the Glory Be. Or you may wish to use your own words to pray. Your prayer should come from your heart. You have already done it, Kari. You talked to God when you offered a special intention for someone.

Kari: You make talking to God sound simple.

Mom: It is simple. God wants to hear from us all the time. Whenever we even whisper a prayer to God, when we're scared or happy or we don't know what to do, we're talking to God and saying, "I love you."

Kari: I get it.

Mom: God wants us to talk to Him about everything — any time and about anything on our minds.

Kari: Do you talk to God like that?

Mom: I sure do. And so does Dad. When we're not feeling good, we pray. And when we're not sure what to do we might pray, "Please help me, Jesus."

Kari: You guys get scared, too?

Mom: Just like everybody else. When we do, we feel much better because we have talked to God.

Kari: I'm going to try that!

Dinnertime Blessings

There is a built-in blessing about the family mealtime which makes it a good place for family prayer. If you are just beginning family prayer, praying at mealtimes is a good place to start.

Sharing a meal, as you already know, is vital to a healthy family life.

What a wonderful and built-in opportunity meals are for parents. Christ calls us to make mealtimes occasions of relaxation, faith-sharing, and togetherness.

Mealtime Is Special Time

Consider the many ways that Christ used food to demonstrate His love. It was no coincidence that Christ began His public ministry and performed His first miracle at a banquet, at the marriage feast at Cana. It was also at dinner that Christ called Matthew, a despised tax collector and sinner. Matthew was to be one of Christ's apostles. There's room at God's table for every repentant sinner.

Later, with the multiplication of the loaves and the fishes, Christ again showed the importance of eating in community (common unity). The meal — though large by any standards — became a unifying and a blessed event. A miracle took place.

Of course, the Last Supper was chosen by Christ as the means to be used by His Church to pass on His real presence through the consecrated bread and wine.

You already know how hard this can be. Mealtimes with small children can be anything but tranquil or predictable. If it's not a fussy baby or spilled milk, it's adolescents juggling piano lessons and paper routes. Or it's sports events or teens with part-time jobs, extra-curricular schedules, or minds of their own.

Yet, as parents, we must remember that this hour in our day is a gift from God. It is a special time of family togetherness and love. It may not be perfect, but we can strive to give it the focus and priority it deserves in a Christian home.

In our family, we have banned problem-solving, TVs, and radios from the mealtime. We have also insisted that there should be no one eating separately unless circumstances or previous plans mandate it.

All of this creates a healthy climate for prayer at the dining room table. Every meal should begin with prayer. Even the food will taste better, and the conversation is guaranteed to be more peaceful.

Suggest that the family thank God for the blessing of rain and sunshine, without which there would be no food. Mealtime is a good time to ask for God's blessing upon the earth. Ask the children to think about a part of the earth they would want God to bless. Mealtime is a good time to think of those who are less fortunate, especially those who go to bed hungry.

In addition to the "Bless Us, O Lord" prayer, our youngsters read or recite another meal prayer of their choice. We keep handy a prayer sheet with some of our favorite "short" prayers.

Remember, meeting together for the evening meal may be the first haven of refuge and relief for parents and children since leaving home in the morning for school and jobs.

With little effort, you can make this opportunity a time of leisure, laughter, and love.

For discussion: Does your family have a favorite mealtime prayer? Invite and encourage your children to make up their own mealtime prayers.

Nighttime Prayers

Nighttime is another ideal time for prayer. In our family, we pray night prayers together. You might want to try it. It is never perfect, but it won't be dull either.

Once, our Dominic, then four, was so anxious to be able to lead the family in our nightly Rosary, he practiced for days. When Dominic got to the Hail Mary, however, it sounded like Our Lady was in the bakery business: "Hail Mary, full of Glaze. . . ."

A bit of humor in the night prayer is not always bad. It's especially good if there's an afraid-to-smile-someone-might-notice-me teen around.

Night prayer provides a good time for special prayer intentions. In our house, we've heard some great ones: "God help get the baby out of Mom's stomach soon." "Please tell the tooth fairy I swallowed it by accident and that it should still count." "Dear Jesus, be sure to tell Santa we got another kid." "Help us find the missing frogs Dominic let loose."

Often, however, husbands and wives do not pray together. So there is no night prayer. It is not because the couple does not want to pray. It's because they feel awkward doing it and are too timid. Children can help get couples over this barrier of self-consciousness in prayer. After all, the souls of our children are at stake. Teaching children to pray can only be done if they see parents doing it.

If you haven't been doing it before, make yourself a promise that praying at night before bedtime will close the day. Never mind the wiggling tot, testy teen, or the endless distractions.

Praying With Scripture

The Sunday Scripture readings provide excellent inspiration for prayer. Can we go wrong with God's Word?

For example, in the fifteenth Sunday of Ordinary Time, cycle C, the Gospel is the parable of the Good Samaritan, Luke 10:29-37. Read the story with your children. Imagine yourself being a person in the story, and invite your children to do the same. Talk about the thoughts and feelings that family members have. Discuss how family members can be "good Samaritans" on the job, in school, in the home, in your neighborhood and community. Then ask God to help your family live the gospel message faithfully.

Through the years, the Kuharskis have seen that something gentle and good occurs when we take time at the end of each day to pray as a family. We all come away a bit transformed and tranquil.

When children are involved, expect reverence — but not perfection. So what if they're wiggly. So what if the phone is ringing or if the toilet is still stopped up.

Take solace in the words of St. Augustine: "the mere intent to pray is itself a prayer." Children will pick up more by osmosis and example than by any sense of fervency they may occasionally experience.

Nighttime prayer together can do these things for your family:

• Put you and your children in a calm prayerful state. It brings an end-of-the-day reminder of the many blessings to be thankful for. Prayers become much more fervent if your children are given a chance to tell what special intentions they have. Treat no intention as frivolous.

• Help settle children down. It puts something sacred and reverent in their thoughts as they end their waking day.

• Give a golden opportunity for children to witness their parents in prayer. If God is important in your lives, He will be important to your children.

• Give opportunities to receive grace from God.

You might find that the Rosary is a powerful prayer for this nighttime visit with God. It takes only ten to fifteen minutes to recite.

Or you might want to make it a time of thanksgiving.

Review with your children the events of the day. Help them to know that just as it is good to say "thank you" to people, so it is with God.

It is not good to go to bed feeling guilt about some part of the day. Nighttime can be a good time to tell God that we're sorry for any ways that we haven't done what we should have. Expressing sorrow can be done individually. But it can have a powerful effect when done as a family. Simply ask: "Is there anything that happened today that bothers you? Or makes you feel sad? Is there something that you wish you had done differently?"

All in all, evening prayer is a unifying experience. Night prayer can seem to lighten a load, relieve tensions, or temper areas of unrest and hurt.

For reflection: Consider giving each other a blessing at the end of the day, including the children blessing the parents. Or you could set aside one day a week to do this as evening prayer. Make the Sign of the Cross on the person's forehead as the words of the blessing are being said. You could say something as simple as, "God bless you" or "I bless you in the name of the Father, and of the Son, and of the Holy Spirit."

Prayers for All Occasions

In his epistles, St. Paul repeatedly reminds us to "pray always" and to "do all things in prayer." When I first read his words, I thought: "I'll bet he never had to contend with a house full of kids." Let Paul wake up to the sound of a dozen eggs dropped on a newly washed kitchen floor. Let Paul get a notice of "head lice" sent home the same day out-of-town company is arriving. Let Paul nurse a house full of toddlers with the twenty-four-hour flu. "Praying always" sounds good in theory. But is it realistic?

When you begin to put prayer into practice, you will begin to understand St. Paul's instruction. Praying and thanking God for all the circumstances of the day has a way of uplifting and encouraging you. It's like singing when you're down. In addition, we are setting a good example for our children. We inspire them to do the same.

Scripture advises us to "Praise God in all things." We can turn every event, even unhappy ones to God. Yes, it's hard to thank God for the bad news as well as the good. But once you get into the habit, it becomes easy.

Catholic Prayers

Here is a list of time-honored prayers in the Catholic tradition.

They are said by many Catholics in groups, as family prayers, and as individual personal prayer.

Our Father	Morning Offering
Amen	Evening Prayer
Sign of the Cross	Grace at Meals
Glory Be to the Father	Prayers for the Dead
Hail Mary	Magnificat
The Rosary	The Angelus
Hail, Holy Queen	Regina Caeli
The Apostles' Creed	Memorare
Acts of Faith, Hope, and Love	Benedictus
Act of Contrition	Prayer to the Holy Spirit
Prayer of Repentance: Miserere	Prayer for the Pope

My kids often hear me whisper a "Thank you, Jesus" or "Praise God" for the sorrows as well as the joys. I may say it through clenched teeth. The occasion could be a fender bender or some unexpected glitch.

Something happens when you turn unpleasant situations over to God with praise. Just being thankful "in all things" reminds us that we are God's children. We refuse to be held hostage or frustrated by any catastrophe thrown our way.

Praising God in all things is an act of faith. It acknowledges that God is in control and truly can, as the Bible says, make "goodness come from all things for those who love the Lord."

Adversity is your opportunity to identify with Jesus in His passion and resurrection. You can offer up joys and sufferings for the love of God and for the benefit of others. And you can teach your children to think and pray in this direction, too. "I'm doing this for you, God." That's a prayer.

You can make your whole day a prayer and offering to God. You can offer each action and activity, no matter how trivial, to God. And you can do it any time, at the moment it occurs to you and later with the family.

For reflection: Think about how the words we use reflect our attitudes. They can also affect our attitudes. Read Psalm 96 or Psalm 148 together as a family. Discuss how the words make you feel. Why do words of praise put a smile in our hearts and maybe even on our faces?

Simulated Conversation: Just Between You and Me

A conversation between a parent and an older child . . .

Dad: Bill, I've noticed that lately you have been backing off when we pray together.

Bill: I don't know what you mean.

Dad: Well, you seem awfully busy with homework or you get tied up with a phone call that just can't wait.

Bill: Well, I've got a lot of things going on.

Dad: Is it hard for you to pray with us?

Bill: Sometimes, but it's not that I don't believe in God.

Dad: I know that. Mom and I are proud of the ways you show your faith. You're becoming a fine young man.

Bill: That's it. I'm growing up. Shouldn't I be able to decide when I pray? I can pray just as well in my room, by myself when I want to do it.

Dad: Do you think it would be easier to pray *by yourself*?

Bill: Yeah!

Dad: Don't you think it would be easy to forget?

Bill: Well, maybe.

Dad: That's one benefit of going to Mass or praying together as a family. We help each other to pray.

Bill: What if someone doesn't feel like praying with others?

Dad: There are times when I'm drained from a bad day at work. I am tired, and sometimes mad —

Bill: I know what you mean. That's how I feel every day after school.

Dad: . . . But I still pray. God asks us to. Prayer shows our love and our obedience to God. Each time you've prayed with the family, or by yourself, when you didn't feel like it, you're showing love and obedience to God.

Bill: It's hard when you don't feel up to it.

Dad: Sure it is. But God *knows* there are times when we don't feel like talking to Him. I like to believe that He blesses us even more at those times.

Bill: I'm not so sure.

Dad: Don't little kids throw tantrums when they don't want to do something?

Bill: Yeah, like Jimmy does.

Dad: Yes. Like a two-year-old, you could have thrown a tantrum. You could have argued with Mom and me, and refused to pray with us. But you didn't. You might have been reluctant, but you were obedient. And for this, your mom and I are even more grateful and proud of you.

Bill: Are you trying to win me over with flattery, Dad?

Dad: No, no! What I'm saying, Bill, is that you are showing your respect and love for Mom and me, because we ask you to be with us. That's called maturity. And you show that to God too.

Bill: I never thought of it that way.

Angels and Saints

Catholics are lucky to have a stockpile of saintly heroes for "all occasions." These heroes are wonderful prayer partners. But the only way our children are going to know about these remarkable individuals is if they meet them first.

That began to happen at our house when I started reading some books about the lives of the saints. Many books for children about saints feature short narrations, colorful pictures, and easy-to-read stories.

Saints are, like you and me, ordinary human beings who did extraordinary things — all for the love of God.

There are those who misunderstand Catholic devotion to the saints and to the Blessed Mother. They mistakenly believe that we are worshiping these men and women in our prayers. That's not true.

Here's the way you could explain this to your children. If you had a special need or project, wouldn't you call your best friend and ask for help? Catholics are doing that in asking other members of our spiritual family — the saints — to pray along with them. That is what is meant by the "Communion of Saints."

As for the angels, I've often told my children, "At baptism, God assigns you your very own Guardian Angel who is here just for you. This angel will never let you stray too long, or allow you to get too far away from God's love, as long as we are faithful."

Christians who ignore the angels and saints cheat themselves out of a most powerful help in prayer.

The closest saint to Christ, of course, is His mother, Mary.

God chose to be born into the world. He chose Mary as His mother. On the Cross, Jesus asked Mary to be our mother. So Mary wants to hear our prayers. She wants to ask Jesus, her Son, to give us what we need.

If your children have biblical or saints' names, you will also want them to feel a special and spiritual kinship to their heavenly hero. Suggest that your child could and should turn to this saint often in prayer.

You can also teach your children that each saint has a special area and mission. I've turned to St. Gerard, patron of pregnant women, when we were expecting our babies — even the adopted ones. I've prayed for my school-age youngsters with the help of St. John Bosco who is known as the "Apostle of Youth." As a mother of many children, I've turned often to Catherine of Siena. She was the twenty-fifth child in her family and became known as one of the finest theological minds of the Church. I pray often to St. Thérèse, the Little Flower. As a cloistered nun, her job was laundress, a job I can relate to. You should also tell your children about St. Jude, the patron saint of "lost causes" and St. Francis of Assisi, the protector of animals.

Once you begin reading about the lives of the saints, you will find your own arsenal of friends who did and continue to do extraordinary things for the love of God.

For discussion: How are saints special in your family? Is there a special saint? During dinnertime, ask family members to share the qualities they would include under "saintliness."

What the Church Says About Prayer

The Christian family is the primary place for education in prayer.

Prayer is a gift of grace and our response to God. Prayer is the life of the heart renewed. In order to pray, one must want to pray.

Christ is the source of prayer. In the Christian life, Christ waits for us in order to enable us to drink from the living waters of the Holy Spirit.

The Church encourages all to learn of the "surpassing knowledge of Christ" by frequent reading of Holy Scripture. Prayer should attend the reading of Scripture so that it may become a conversation between God and the person.

The Liturgy is a source of prayer when it is interiorized and assimilated during and after its celebration.

Through faith and prayer we seek and desire the face of God, wanting to hear and keep His word. Love is the source of prayer, whoever draws from it reaches the summit of prayer.

The Church invites us to invoke the Holy Spirit as the interior master of Christian prayer. The way of Christian prayer is Christ. There is no access to God, the Father, unless prayed in the name of Jesus.

Because of Mary's singular cooperation with the action of the Holy Spirit, the Church likes to pray in communion with her, centering on the person of Christ. Mary, the figure of the Church, is the perfect "pray-er." We can pray with and to Mary. The Church's prayer is sustained by Mary's and united with it in hope.

The Church invites all people to regular prayer each day through personal prayer, the Liturgy of the Hours, Sunday Eucharist, the feasts of the liturgical year.

The Christian tradition has three major expressions of the life of prayer: vocal prayer, meditation, and discursive prayer. They have in common the recollection of the heart.

Prayer and the Christian life are inseparable. Prayer is a vital necessity.

Because of the challenges to overcome the self and the culture, prayer is at times a struggle.

Jesus, before He died, prayed to the Father. This prayer (see John 17) is called the priestly prayer and sums up the whole economy of creation and salvation. It inspires the great petitions of the Our Father.

In response to His disciples' request, "Lord, teach us to pray" (Luke 11:1), Jesus entrusted them with the fundamental Christian prayer, the Our Father.

The Lord's prayer is the summary of the whole Gospel. It is at the very heart of the Scriptures. It is the most perfect of prayers.

Death and the Afterlife
Robert Barr

To Die Is to Gain

For to me life is Christ, and death is gain (Philippians 1:21).

Death is scary. Death is also the passage to a life lovely beyond describing.

Children deserve to know about the loveliness. As human beings, steeped in the human condition, they already "know" enough about the scary side — death as the dark terror within us, especially deep in our "unconscious," that we inherit from the countless generations since Adam.

The prospect of their own death one day, and the deaths of those around them that they may already have begun to experience, powerfully assault their consciousness. In some tragic instances, children will know of their own terminal diseases . . . their own deaths in the offing.

The heart of the matter — the gift of faith

God has promised us a perfect existence, and therefore an endless one. The perfect, everlasting creator of the universe has created the universe only for love, so that the persons in it may be able to imitate God's love and so attain salvation. Nor has God set any limits on that love that we are to have — not even limits of time. This is why God has willed us to have an endless existence.

God could not have been satisfied with simply loving us — without loving us forever.

Why did the eternal God create the universe? To share love with other beings. What utter nonsense, then, that the eternal God would want these beings to be temporary!

Death ends human life on earth as a time in which we receive or reject God's life and love offered to us in Jesus. Scripture affirms the immediate reward after death of each one of us according to our behavior. The parable of the poor man, Lazarus, (see Luke 16:22) and Christ's words to the good thief (see Luke 23:43) illustrate this truth. Living faith makes us long for eternal life as Paul says, "We would rather leave the body and go home to the Lord" (2 Corinthians 5:8).

This knowledge is part of the most precious gift we can transmit to our children: the gift of faith, which is always accompanied by hope and love.

For reflection: How do you feel about death? What is your faith concerning life after death?

Special Things to Remember

The key element in talking to your children about death and the afterlife is a sense of utter realism about the afterlife.

This will not always be easy. After all, no one on earth has seen the afterlife. So the danger is that, by a kind of domino effect, as your children grow up, the Christian doctrine of death and the afterlife could go the way of Santa Claus and the Easter bunny. It has happened to many a Christian. You want to be clear with your children about the reality of the afterlife, from their young age onward.

Images of the afterlife

But *how* are you to communicate your faith in the utter reality of the afterlife to your children? How can you describe something that no one has ever seen or experienced?

Through images of beautiful things in this present life.

Just take any good thing — ice cream, the love of the person you love most, or anything in between — and multiply by a thousand thousand thousand, and you will have some small inkling of the beauty of the afterlife.

The following are some categories of images that will be appropriate for every age. In the following pages, we will suggest concrete imagery of eternity which are appropriate for different age levels.

Images of forever: A "world without end," as in the Christian liturgy (*saecula saeculorum*: literally, "centuries of centuries," or "hundreds of hundreds of years").

Not a falling asleep: Rather, a waking up. Not a lapsing into unconsciousness, as in sleep, but precisely an enormous enhancement of our consciousness.

Organic fruition: Our afterlife will be the eternal life of precisely the person we have become in this life. If we become improvers of the world around us, and thus hasten the coming of the reign of God, we shall be precisely such people — lovers in the everlasting reign of God.

Steeped in God: To live in the afterlife is like being a sponge awash in an infinite ocean, an ocean of God, without surface, bottom, or shores.

Coping with the fear of death

Besides conveying the utter reality of the afterlife, another very challenging task you face in talking to your children about death and the afterlife is helping them surmount the fear that the notion of death arouses.

Death is an annihilation. It is the annihilation of everything that cannot inherit eternal life. One of the things that cannot inherit eternal life is our limited consciousness of reality. So we rightly fear death, as consciousness is in our present life and something we know.

But this fear need not be terror. To fear death as something unknown, as a leap in the dark, is healthy. But to be terrified of this "in the dark" is not Christian.

What can you do to prevent your children's healthy fear and respect of death as a leap into the unknown from becoming the terror of persons who have no hope?

You can help your children make the "leap" of faith, as it has been called — the leap that is God's gift to us in the present moment, to prepare us for the leap in the dark that is death.

In order to make this leap of faith, and help your children to make it, you need to focus on the utter reality of the afterlife. At the same time, you must face the fear of death in your children.

How can you effectively face the fear of death with your children?

One very important way is by acceptance of the myriad "mini-deaths" that you undergo as you move through the present life. These mini-deaths are meant to prepare you for the real thing: your actual death.

The mightiest mini-deaths are the "passages" of life. Birth is the first — that shock of cold air and having to face the "reality of the world" for the first time.

Other mini-deaths include the passage from infancy to later childhood, when you began to have responsibilities; the passage to adolescence, with its raging hormones and traumatic new challenges; the passage from adolescence to adulthood, when you suddenly had to meet your responsibilities on your own; the "mid-life crisis," when you subconsciously feel that you have reached the noontime of your life and have peeked down the other side of the clock of life; the passage to old age — called senior citizenship to soften the blow — when, deep down inside, you fear being thrust aside as having lived out your usefulness, and begin to wonder whether you're "as good as dead" already.

All of these life passages, accepted correctly, can help you deal with the fear of death. Your children have already experienced some of them.

Commonplace, everyday experiences of life, too, are mini-deaths. The list is endless: the death of a child, spouse, or friend; the sense of desperation that comes with alcoholism or other drug addiction; a friend's betrayal or a failed love relationship; physical or emotional illness; failure in school or in the workplace; sex or race discrimination; marital tension; the suffering of children; the pain of the generation gap; world poverty and hunger; war or the fear of war; loneliness. These mini-deaths also prepare you for the real thing.

Besides having made the great passages of birth and early childhood, your children have already suffered some of the commonplace mini-deaths.

Your heart would break if you heard your little child say, as I heard my own child say, "Aw, I'm just a stupid little kid." That exquisite "little kid" has already "died" — in a small, but oh so traumatic, way. The pain of an illness, the death of a pet, the death of a loved one, rejection by a friend — even our children's mini-deaths are many.

Bereavement and grieving

Realism about the perfection of the afterlife must not be allowed to interfere with grieving on the part of the bereaved. Grief at another person's death is an integral part of love, including Christian love. The bereaved are genuinely deprived of a good, and the greatest created good that exists, another person.

Jesus knew what it meant to lose a loved one. He wept at the tomb of Lazarus and groaned over the loss which death brings. At the same time, He performed the miracle of raising Lazarus from the dead and witnessed the truth of immortality and eternal life. God promises that our grieving will end in eternal life. "God will wipe away every tear from their eyes" (Revelation 7:17).

For reflection: What images work best for you in describing the afterlife? What mini-deaths have you experienced in your life? How have they affected your attitude about life?

'Is Ray Planted?'
Ideas for Preschool and Primary-Grade Children

Images of the afterlife

Here are some ways of expressing images of the afterlife for young children.

Fun: How would you like to have fun all day, every bit of the day, and have the day never end?

Activities: How would you like to be able to do your favorite activities any time you wanted to?

Friends: How would you like to play with your best friend anytime doing your favorite thing together?

Family: How would you like to close your eyes, and suddenly open them again and see your family running to hug you and never have to leave them again?

Games: How would you like to be able to play with any game you wanted any time you wanted to?

Planting and sprouting: After a family friend had died, and my wife, Marilyn, and I had attended the funeral without our little Margaret — Margaret, then four, asked, when we'd returned home, "Is Ray planted?" She meant, "Has he been buried?" Marilyn had made sure that her young ears had always heard Christian burial as a planting for resurrection. Jesus used the image of planting just like four-year-old Margaret, "Unless a grain of wheat falls to the ground and dies, it remains just a grain of wheat. But if it dies, it produces much fruit" (John 12:24). And St. Paul had the same idea: "In an instant, in the blink of an eye, . . . the dead will be raised . . . and that which is mortal must clothe itself with immortality" (1 Corinthians 15:52-53).

Images of forever: Our life with God after we die will be like living so long that you'll have had a thousand birthdays — and that's just the beginning!

Images of excitement: What's the happiest and most excited you ever were? Well, our life in God will be a thousand times more exciting even than that!

Coping with the fear of death

This is the age at which children may first reflect on their experience of the death of someone or something they love. Mister Rogers advises that when a pet dies is often when kids first wonder, "What *is* dying?" If your child doesn't raise the question, you can bring it up, and present the Christian perspective on death and the afterlife. But remember that when a pet dies, your child may want time to be alone.

Bereavement and grieving

The bereaved weep. Sometimes they sob. Children must know that they may weep and even sob. Why? Because they have really lost the most precious thing there is: another person (or a pet).

Explain to them that Mommy and Daddy cried, too, when Grandma died.

But explain to them as well that the person who has died hasn't lost you. She is perfectly well aware of you, and clasps you to her heart. You've lost her, that's true. So you're right to be sad. Of course, one day, after your own death, you'll be with her again. Meanwhile, be glad for her: She has you with her already, right now. She sees you and loves you right now.

Simulated Conversation: A Really Exciting Life

The three simulated conversations in this chapter are meant to provide encouragement, increase the comfort level, and spark the imagination of parents in discussing death and the afterlife with their children.

A conversation between a parent and a child from four or five years old to seven or eight years old . . .

Margaret: I'm scared, Mommy.

Mom: Really? Of what?

Margaret: Of when I'm going to die.

Mom: So is everybody, Margaret. I am too. And I'm a lot closer to it than you!

Margaret: You too, Mommy? You're scared?

Mom: In a way. Death is scary. Because you can't see the other side. If you could see the other side, it wouldn't be scary.

Margaret: What's on the other side?

Mom: The other side of death? It's called the afterlife. It's when you live again, after you die.

Margaret: Where?

Mom: Who knows where. That's one of the things we can't see. But somewhere. And it'll be terrifically fun.

Margaret: Really?

Mom: Sure! How would you like to be able to play with your friends all day, every bit of the day, and never get tired and have the day never end?

Margaret: Yes! But I'll miss you and Daddy and Katie.

Mom: No you won't. We'll be right there. When you die, you skip over time, all the way to the time when everyone else dies too. So we'll all be right there.

Margaret: And hug me?

Mom: And hug you.

Margaret: And I won't be lonely?

Mom: Not for a single instant.

Our faith says we believe in the "Communion of Saints." We have a community of friends in heaven who are united with the community of the faithful on earth. The love of the Holy Spirit binds us together. The saints love us and pray for us.

You'll Never Want to Come Back: Ideas for Intermediate-Grade Children

Images of the afterlife

At the intermediate age, many children attend the funeral of a family friend for the first time. A willingness and openness to talk about it can be of great help to your child. You need not force a conversation. There will be moments when your child needs to be alone, to do his or her own reflecting. You need only say, "Anything you want to talk about, about Joe and his funeral? Just let me know."

Perhaps some of the following images may be helpful in talking with your children about the afterlife and about death, the passage to that life.

Images of forever. A Hindu legend has it that, every thousand years, a wonderful bird flies across the world, and in the course of his flight touches with his wing one of the peaks of the Himalayas. When the Himalayas are completely worn away by the successive touches of that bird's wing, eternity will be just getting started.

Birth. A TV documentary portrayed a beautiful way a parent explained to her grade-school child, who (it was thought at the time) was dying of cancer, what to expect at death.

In effect, she said: "When you were born, you screamed and cried. You didn't want to be born. But now, would you want to go back into the womb?"

"No," came the child's reply, "of course not."

"Well," the parent went on, "that's how it is with death. You don't *want* to cross over, because you've never been there and never seen how it is. That's why it's scary to die. And it's all right to be scared. But would you like to know something? Once you've crossed over, you'll never want to come back. It's too lovely there. And all your family and friends will run to join you when they themselves die."

Bereavement and grieving

Death is a fearsome thing for a person about to die, and a devastation for the bereaved — those suddenly bereft of this person. On the other hand, death is also a relief from hardship and suffering. Talk about it in the sense of the freedom it confers.

"Do you remember how Uncle Charlie was so sick before he died? Well, he isn't sick any more. He's happy again."

Simulated Conversation: Your Kind of Afterlife: It's Up to You

A conversation between a parent and an intermediate-grade child . . .

Margaret: Dad, how do you know if you're going to heaven?

Dad: Well, do you think you're going someplace else?

Margaret: Couldn't I go to hell or purgatory? We're learning about them, too!

Dad: Well, I suppose you could. It's up to you.

Margaret: Up to me! How?

Dad: Well . . . are you a lover or a hater?

Margaret: A lover, I guess. Maybe a hater sometimes. I don't know.

Dad: But is there anyone you will hate forever, and try to hurt as much as possible?

Margaret: No, not that much.

Dad: Then you don't hate them. You only dislike them. Don't ever try to hurt someone in a very serious way that can never be repaired. Then that will eliminate hell. That leaves purgatory and heaven. Is your love for people strong or weak?

Margaret: I don't know. How can you tell?

Dad: Well, by whether you try to do a lot for people, even when it costs you effort, and sometimes even suffering; or whether you only do as little as possible for people.

Margaret: Well, sometimes a lot, sometimes a little.

Dad: Then you'll go to purgatory, followed by heaven.

Margaret: I don't want to go to purgatory! There's fire there.

Dad: No, there isn't. It's true, the souls in purgatory hurt — but their only hurt is the hurt of being sorry they didn't do more for people. A whole book was written about the joys of the souls in purgatory.

Margaret: What? You mean they're glad they're in purgatory?

Dad: Well, I suppose so. After all, the only way out of purgatory is to heaven. If you're in purgatory, you can never go to hell. The souls in purgatory are saved. So besides being sorry for not having been better persons, they are enormously glad.

Margaret: Because they're saved?

Dad: Also because in purgatory God uses their sorrow for not having been more loving toward people to show them how God loves them, and invites them to love people in the same way from now on, forever.

Margaret: Wow! But by the way, where are heaven and hell and purgatory, anyway?

Dad: Well, they aren't anywhere, actually.

Margaret: You mean, they aren't real?

Dad: Oh, they're real, all right. But they aren't places. How could you be in a place, when you've left your body and died? They're experiences. They're nicknames for experiences of God. And they happen at death. Heaven is swimming in the fun of God — God going through you making you happy. Hell is only for people who are deliberately and totally bad, swimming in the thought that they could have done what God wanted and they deliberately and totally didn't want to. They decided to be a hater. Purgatory is God going through you in such a way that you wish you had loved everybody as best you could, not only in big ways, but in the tiniest ways, too. And the good news is, now you get a chance to. Everybody is soaked in God in one of these ways at the moment of death.

Margaret: So it depends on me.

Dad: It depends on you. And God, your best friend, guarantees you the grace to be able to live in such a way that, when you come to die, in that same instant you'll open your eyes and you'll be in . . .

Margaret: Heaven?

Dad: Heaven. I think I know you, Margaret. You're a person who . . .

Margaret: Who'll be doing things for people?

Dad: Who'll be doing things for people.

See 1 Corinthians 15:35-58 for an excellent shared prayer text for parents and their children.

You Deserve a Good Afterlife: Ideas for Junior-High Children

Shocking as it often is to parents, children of this age feel a deep self-doubt. You must be careful not to encourage a contempt for this life on the basis of the superiority of the afterlife. The afterlife is a product of the organic fruition of this life. We shall be, in the next life, what we become in this one.

The most serious danger of emphasizing the perfection of the afterlife is ironically the danger of suicide. Suicide can be seen by some young adolescents as a permanent solution for a temporary problem.

It has been said that when one has a "difficulty of faith," the real difficulty — the difficulty masquerading as a difficulty of faith — is a difficulty of love. The person who suffers temptations against faith is really feeling, deep inside, perhaps unconsciously, that she or he is not loved.

It happens to everyone. But it happens often, perhaps most devastatingly, to young people. This is worth remembering if your young adolescent tells you, "I don't believe [in God, in heaven, in my religion, etc.] any more!"

Young adolescents need to know that they deserve a better afterlife than the one they would have if they haven't lived this life out to the fullest. The mature, experienced, courageous person they are now is precisely the person they will be in the afterlife, multiplied a thousandfold.

Images of the afterlife

Junior-high age is the time to share with your child a vivid image of Christ rising from the dead and sweeping us along with Him. A great crowd of persons rise together with Jesus, ignoring the limitations of time and space to join Him in His resurrection nearly two thousand years ago.

Images of the social: Generally, and in keeping with this same image of joining Jesus in His resurrection, social images will be appropriate at this age. All-night parties (where the chaperon will be God, the one having the most fun), dances, soccer games, are the types of images young adolescents will relate to.

Images of human perfection: Children of this age are specially responsive to an appeal to their idealism. Images of human perfection are therefore appropriate here, such as the happiest day you've ever had, or people treating each other with utter kindness, respect, and consideration.

Images of forever: Scientific facts begin to have a special appeal at this age. Light travels 186,000 miles per second — or what we term "instantaneously." And yet the nearest star is four light-years away. The entire universe is billions of light-years across. When light will have traveled from one corner of the universe to the opposite corner, eternity will have just begun.

Coping with the fear of death

Your child may begin to have doubts of faith for reasons discussed above. The agnostic, scientific culture of our modern age may influence your child with a kind of "scientism," or feeling that nothing is worth saying except the raw facts of scientific analysis.

The best approach will doubtless be to admit that you doubt sometimes. Then help your child overcome the doubt not only by an appeal to love (which helps them to get out of themselves), but by presenting as scientific an explanation of the afterlife as you can.

You could remind the child of the Church's modern approach to funerals. The funeral Mass is called the Mass of the Resurrection, and the garments of the presiders are all white. The funeral Mass celebrates, commemorates in advance, the resurrection of the deceased person.

In the same spirit, the Sacrament of the Anointing of the Sick should be talked about as a moment of God's comfort and strengthening of a sick person. It is conferred in order to assure the person anointed, who may or may not be at the point of death, that everything will be all right.

"Remember when Grandpa lived with us a while before he died? Remember how the priest came in one night to anoint him with oil as a guarantee that God would be with him and everything would be all right? And remember how much easier that made it for Grandpa to leave us — both for him and for us?"

Bereavement and grieving

Just as people are right to fear death without being terrorized by it, so also people are right to cry at Masses of Resurrection celebrated at funerals, or at the conferral of the Sacrament of the Sick on a person actually dying. But as your child will now begin to experience, the weeping that believers do for their departed is a unique, profound experience of mixed feelings. We are sad for ourselves. We may even be sad for the person who has died, because we wish he or she had lived longer or happier. But we are happy about the afterlife of the person of whom we are bereft.

Simulated Conversation: The Promise

A conversation between parent and a junior-high child . . .

Ted: Hey, Mom. What are we when we die? Just meat?

Mom: Of course not.

Ted: What do you mean, "Of course not"? Dead people look like just meat.

Mom: Sure, but they aren't.

Ted: How do you know?

Mom: The Creator of everything made sure they wouldn't be.

Ted: But how do you know?

Mom: God promised the resurrection of our bodies.

Ted: Is that in the Bible?

Mom: Yes, it is. Remember the story of the resurrection of Lazarus — and even the resurrection of Christ's body?

Ted: And is that real Catholic faith?

Mom: Yes, our Catholic faith, which we received from our parents and desire to pass on to you, teaches that when we die our souls remain alive and one day we will get back our resurrected bodies.

Ted: Does the Bible promise the resurrection of my body?

Mom: Absolutely. Jesus promised that God would raise our bodies from the dead.

Ted: When?

Mom: Who knows? Maybe a hundred years, maybe a million. When our heavenly Father wills it.

Ted: A million years? You mean I'll have to wait that long to come back to life?

Mom: There's no waiting. Time stops when you're dead. Stops still. So the moment you close your eyes in death, you open them again to your new life in eternity. Remember, your soul lives on.

Ted: So my soul lives on. . . . And for my body it's like going into a time machine and instantly moving ahead a couple of hundred years? Or million? Until the resurrection of the body?

Mom: Exactly.

Ted: When God is ready, huh?

Mom: When the Father is ready.

Ted: When will that be?

Mom: Jesus tells us that no one knows. It's here in the Bible: "But of that day and hour no one knows, neither the angels of heaven, nor the Son, but the Father alone" (Matthew 24:36). Son, it is in heaven that we finally reach our ultimate happiness. It is in heaven that "God will wipe away every tear from our eyes" (Revelation 7:17).

What the Church Says About Death and the Afterlife

Christians who unite their own deaths to that of Jesus view it as the final step toward Him and the gateway into everlasting life.

After death, a particular judgment follows in which each of our lives is evaluated in relation to Christ and we receive — in our immortal souls — eternal recompense: purification or immediate entry into the blessings of heaven or into everlasting damnation.

Heaven is the ultimate end and fulfillment of humanity's deepest longings, the state of supreme and final happiness. Heaven is perfect communion of life and love with the Most Holy Trinity, the Virgin Mary, the angels, and the blessed. To live in heaven is to be with Christ. Those in heaven live in Him, but they retain, or rather find, their true identity, their own name. This mystery of blessed fellowship with God and all who are in Christ surpasses all understanding and description. The beatific vision is God's opening to us His sacred mystery to our immediate contemplation, giving us the ability to see God in heavenly glory.

All who die in God's grace and friendship are assured of eternal salvation. Those among the dead not yet perfectly purified undergo a purification after death, so as to obtain the holiness necessary to enter the joy of heaven. This purification is known as purgatory. The Church has always honored the memory of the dead and offered prayers, especially the eucharistic sacrifice, for them so that, purified, they may attain the beatific vision of God. The Church also commends almsgiving, indulgences, and works of penance on their behalf.

We cannot be united to God unless we freely choose to love Him. But we cannot love God if we gravely sin against Him, against our neighbor, or even against ourselves. To die in mortal sin without repenting and accepting God's merciful love is to remain separated from Him forever by our own free choice. The Church definitely teaches the existence and eternity of hell. God does not predestine anyone to hell. A voluntary turning away from God and persistence in such mortal sin until the end would be necessary to merit condemnation.

The resurrection of all the dead, of the righteous and the unrighteous, will precede the Last Judgment. In the presence of Christ, the true relationship of each person to God will be fully disclosed. The Last Judgment will reveal what good each has done or failed to do during his or her earthly life. The message of the Last Judgment summons us to conversion while God still gives us the acceptable time, the day of salvation.

Thus, at the end of time, God's kingdom will come in its fullness. Then the just will reign with Christ forever, glorified in body and soul, and the material universe will be transformed. God will then be "all in all" (1 Corinthians 15:28) in eternal life.

Because Children Learn By Doing...
Hands-On Help For Sacramental Preparation!

Called to His Supper: A Preparation for First Eucharist
By Jeannine Timko Leichner
No. 138, Child's Book, $3.95
No. 140, Parent/Teacher Guide, $11.95
Help your children prepare for First Holy Communion with fun projects that offer many opportunities for family involvement.

Making Things Right: The Sacrament of Reconciliation
By Jeannine Timko Leichner
No. 351, English edition, $3.95
No. 349, Spanish edition, $3.95
This best-selling preparation for first reception of the Sacrament of Penance emphasizes God's constant and forgiving love.

Joy, Joy the Mass: Our Family Celebration
By Jeannine Timko Leichner
No. 350, English edition, $2.95
No. 348, Spanish edition, $2.95
Joy, Joy the Mass helps children learn about the central celebration of the Faith by participating in exciting, fun-filled activities.